What Really Works for Children with AUTISM

Peter Vermeulen & Kobe Vanroy

What Really Works for Children with AUTISM

All marketing and publishing rights guaranteed to and reserved by:

(817) 277-0727
(817) 277-2270 (fax)
E-mail: info@fhautism.com
www.fhautism.com

ISBN: 978-1-957984-96-4

CONTENTS

FOREWORD

This book aims to be a guide for anyone who is raising a child with autism, whether at home or in the classroom.

A lot of difficulties with these children arise from a lack of knowledge about exactly what autism is and what its consequences are, which often leads them to be unfairly viewed as odd, lazy, unmotivated, contrary, or naughty. That the needs behind their behavior are not seen or understood causes or reinforces many of these difficulties. The people around these children do not always respond appropriately (often unwillingly), and the children themselves are also not given the right tools to do things differently.

This guide was written to give you accurate and detailed information about what autism is, what the most important needs of these children are, how you can meet them in their sometimes strange or difficult behavior, and how you, as a family, teacher, therapist, or counselor can support them in the right way. You will find many practical tools in this book to help you persevere and give your best every day to guide these children.

You won't recognize everything: each child with autism is unique and also has a lot of characteristics other than those that only belong to autism, which makes the typical features either more or less noticeable.

As you learn more about the specific characteristics, difficulties, and needs of children with autism, their behavior comes into focus in a different light. What you first thought of as difficult

Children with autism are beautiful children with valuable qualities.

behavior turns out to be very human and often a way of dealing with a world not made for their atypical brains. This insight will help you adapt (read: make autism-friendly) your own behavior and the physical environment at home and in the classroom. You can use it to prevent or reduce problems. This often leads to a positive change in the child's behavior.

Difficulties exist with social contact and communication. Along with a more straightforward way of thinking and acting— these main characteristics of autism will always be present, but you can work with the child to ensure they experience less of these characteristics.

Children with autism are wonderful children with valuable qualities, but these are often overshadowed by the difficulties they encounter. This guide will help you to avoid stumbling blocks, tackle challenges, and appeal to children's strengths. As a result, they can (again) develop a fine relationship with themselves, with you as a parent or teacher and with other important people in their lives.

Peter Vermeulen and Kobe Vanroy

HOW TO USE THIS BOOK

In this book, you will find out exactly what autism is and also what it is not. You will discover what really works in dealing with children with autism, so they feel good about themselves and therefore can cope better with their environment and with what you expect of them. We start with ten major needs of these children. For each need, you can read why it is so important and which concrete strategies can help meet it. Then follows a treasury of tips and examples that can support you as a parent at home, but also as an educator, principal, or teacher at school.

It is helpful to go through the book all the way from front to back first. Then you will have a nice overview of the whole picture. In doing so, you will find that the first three needs are the basis for the needs that follow.

After that, use the book as a working tool. Think about which needs might need a little more attention. Try the strategies and tips and evaluate whether each works for you and the child.

Maybe you are already applying some of the tips, or maybe you are still at the start of this journey. Either way, give yourself and the child time to grow into this new approach. That way, you slowly but surely build a toolbox that you can use flexibly, depending on the situation. Above all, do what works for you and the child. Be creative with the tips, bend them to your ambitions, and adapt them to your specific situation. What really works with children with autism is always customized. Hang in there and have faith in a good outcome. Together, we will succeed. In the end, everyone

Together we will succeed.

has the same goal, both the child with autism and the people around them who help the child grow up and develop: that the child is allowed to be themself; gets a good, solid connection with themself and with the significant others around them; and feels they can mean something to this world.

We would like to mention that whenever we use the word autism, we are referring to the full spectrum.

WHAT IS AUTISM?

BEHAVIORAL CHARACTERISTICS

Autism is the name of a group of behavioral traits that result from a brain that interacts with both the outside world and the inside world (one's own body) in an atypical way. Scientists have studied these behavioral traits.

The following are characteristics of the behavior of children with autism:

- **Persistent difficulties in social communication and interaction:**
  - There are difficulties in social-emotional interaction. For example, these children show little or no response to playing together and exploring, have little or no interaction with other children, have difficult interactions because they do not respond correctly to others, are impatient when they have to wait for their turn, or have problems sharing when playing together.
  - These children pick up non-verbal communicative behavior with difficulty or not at all. They do not understand body language well and/or interpret facial expressions with difficulty or not at all and therefore make less use of it themselves.
  - They have difficulties in establishing, maintaining, and understanding relationships, such as making friends or seeing the distinction between friends and acquaintances or between the roles of parents and teachers.

- **Limited, repetitive patterns of behavior, limited interests and activities:**
  - These children show stereotyped or repetitive movements and use objects or speech in stereotyped ways, such as fluttering, rocking, and babbling.
  - They can stick to the same thing and are rigidly attached to routines or rituals, such as doing the same thing every day after coming home from school, before going to bed, and before starting an exercise in class.
  - They have limiting, fixated interests that are unusual in intensity or focus. For example, they are very often concerned with the same thing or want to talk a lot about one particular topic.
  - They respond too much or too little to sensory stimuli or have an unusual interest in the sensory aspects of the environment.

Many scientists call autism a developmental disorder because the atypical functioning of the brain is present from birth and from then on affects the development of many life skills, such as getting along with others, communication, and play.

There is an additional requirement for an autism diagnosis: the behavioral characteristics described here must be present from earliest infancy. This does not mean that they are always recognized at this young age. It does mean that one cannot develop autism later in life.

You also can't be a little autistic if you recognize a particular behavioral characteristic in yourself. All characteristics must be present together. Another additional condition for autism is that the characteristics must result in significant limitations in functioning in many important areas of life, such as schooling, communication, leisure time, and often even eating and sleeping.

Although you see the behavioral characteristics described in all children with autism, you can't really make a list of specific autistic behaviors. The concrete way in which the difficulties in social communication and interaction manifest themselves can be very different. For example, there are children with autism who are very aloof in social contact and even reject contact. But there are also children who very actively seek social contact, but in unusual and sometimes even disruptive ways. Although all children with autism react unusually to sensory stimuli, their sensory profile is unique: not all of these children react too strongly to sound, for example, or dislike being touched.

So there is no such thing as typical autistic behavior. Because these children all have other characteristics in addition to their autism, the concrete behaviors you see in each child can be quite different.

To accommodate that diversity, the official term for autism is now *autism spectrum disorder*, where the word spectrum, like the color spectrum, refers to the various colors that autism can take on. It is not that there are different forms of autism, although you hear that sometimes. What is true is that every child with autism has numerous characteristics, such as intelligence, age, and character, in addition to autism. All of these characteristics combine to create a unique mix and thus the mutual differences in behavior seen in children with autism.

Every child with autism has, in addition to autism, many other features that together provide a unique mix of behavior.

HOW COMMON IS AUTISM?

Autism occurs in 1 in 165 children, possibly slightly more, maybe even up to 1 percent. That means that there is bound to be a child with autism on every street or in every school. You often see higher numbers, especially on the Internet, but it's best to take those with a grain of salt.

Autism is probably not more common than it used to be, but it is diagnosed more often and at younger ages. On average, the diagnosis is made at age 5. Looking only at children, the average age of diagnosis is even lower: 3.5 years.

The fact that it is diagnosed more often and more quickly today is due to several things:

- Society has become more complex. There are increasing demands for flexibility and social and communicative skills, which means that children with autism who could function in the fixed structures of, say, one hundred years ago no longer can.
- There is much more knowledge about autism than there was a few decades ago. The characteristics of autism are more widely known, and childcare providers and teachers, for example, are more likely to express suspicion of autism.
- For many forms of care and support (e.g., special education), a diagnoses is necessary.

- The perception of autism is no longer as extremely negative as it was in the last century. There is also increasing openness to neurodiversity, the fact that there is a lot of variation in how brains work.

About four in ten children with autism also have intellectual disabilities. Autism also accompanies other developmental and brain conditions, such as ADHD, a language development disorder, or epilepsy, more often than usual.

Like all other developmental disorders, autism is more common in boys than in girls. In girls, autism is usually diagnosed later than in boys, especially in girls who are normally to highly gifted. They try hard to be "normal" and are more successful at masking their limitations.

The image of autism is fortunately better than it used to be.

WHAT ARE THE CAUSES OF AUTISM?

Heredity plays an important role in the development of autism, but the genetic story is very complex. Autism cannot be linked to one specific gene or piece of DNA. More than a thousand potentially implicated genes have now been found, and something seems to be going on in more than two thousand pieces of DNA. Moreover, the genetic abnormalities discovered seem to overlap to a large extent with those of other developmental disorders, such as ADHD.

Because autism is largely hereditary, there is a good chance that the child's sibling also displays characteristics of autism. Indeed, as a parent, you may recognize much of yourself. On the one hand, this can be confrontational and can awaken old pain from your own childhood. On the other hand, it can also help you to understand what didn't work in the past and why you sometimes reacted differently from other children. Recognizing traces of autism in yourself or your children does not necessarily mean that you all have autism. Even if you are not diagnosed, the strategies described further in this book can be tools for you or your children. Many autism-friendly tips work equally well for children, adolescents, and adults who are not diagnosed or do not even have autism.

Heredity is not the only element on the list of causes of autism. Environmental factors also seem to play a role. No, this is not about the parents' parenting style. If one thing is clear, it is that you cannot become autistic from a lack of love or from neglect or pampering. For environmental factors, do think about all kinds of environmental influences during pregnancy and/or childbirth: vitamin deficiency, stress, infections during pregnancy, or lack of oxygen during birth.

The specific cause in one child is often impossible to identify.

If one thing is clear, it is that you cannot become autistic from a lack of love or from neglect or pampering.

AUTISM IS A DEVELOPMENTAL CONDITION

To start with, autism is innate. In some children you can see the characteristics of autism early in their development, for example, because they do not follow their parents' eye gaze, because they cry very little or a lot, or because they are not curious about their surroundings. In other children, autism only begins to be noticed later, for example in preschool, when their atypical manner of playing (such as putting everything in rows or spinning everything), their unusual reactions to sound or light, or their problems in contact with other children become apparent. And in still other children, autism surfaces even later, when, for example, they do not succeed in friendship relationships, they do not seem to understand school instructions or understand them very differently, or they have unusual interests or hobbies. For some children, it takes even longer. Their difficulties become apparent only when they drop out of group work, independent work, or internships in secondary education.

Autism does not stop at age eighteen. Although we can do a lot to positively influence and encourage the development of children with autism, autism does not go away. You cannot outgrow autism. Autism does not fade; at most it takes on a different color. The difficulties in social contact, the misunderstandings in communication, the need for clarity and predictability, and the sensory problems are also seen in adults with autism.

However, it is true that many adults with autism, especially those of average to high intelligence, have learned all kinds of tricks and strategies that make them less noticeable and, above all, less affected by their difficulties. It is therefore very important to teach children and their environment how to cope with autism as early as possible so that the negative impact of the difficulties can be minimized and they don't have to mask their difficulties. Masking for a very long term often leads to a so-called autistic burnout.

Autism does not fade; at most it takes on a different color.

AN AUTISTIC BRAIN IS ABSOLUTE AND PRECISE

In a child with autism, the brain works differently. The behavioral characteristics of autism result from a brain that works differently than a typical brain. Autism is not located in one specific area of the brain. Autism exists primarily in how that brain processes information.

To help us respond quickly and efficiently, our brain has learned not to wait until it has gathered all the information about our current situation but to anticipate the situation in advance. Our brain makes predictions about what's ahead of us, so we don't have to process all kinds of information first (What do we see? What do we hear? Who else is here? Where are we?) before reacting. For example, if you are crossing a street at a green pedestrian light, your brain expects the light to turn red, possibly even before you reach the other side. That expectation causes all your muscles to already be ready to accelerate as soon as the light turns red. That's more efficient than not getting going until it turns red. (Aha, the traffic light changes color! What color is this, and what should I do next?)

So our brain is constantly predicting. And it does so based on the knowledge it gathered from previous experiences. For example, the brain has knowledge about traffic lights, including the knowledge that traffic lights usually don't wait to change color until you reach the other side of the street. And your brain has also learned that people don't always respect the rules, so sometimes you do cross at a red light. What your brain also knows is that this is not actually allowed, but that everyone does it and it's okay, as long as no cars are approaching.

Autistic brains, like other brains, also want to be prepared for what lies ahead, so they also predict. Only, in this they differ from non-autistic brains, as they can be sticklers for predictions, and the knowledge they rely on to predict is both absolute and less context sensitive.

For example, Otto goes shopping with his mom. As always, afterward they go to a hamburger restaurant. Otto really likes hamburgers with fries. He also likes the ice cream he always gets. But today Mommy is in a hurry. There is not enough time to get the whole menu at the burger joint, including the ice cream. When Otto notices that there is no ice cream, he has a meltdown. He is very angry with Mom. A child without autism would most likely also not like the fact that the ice cream is missing this time, but they probably would have already noticed that Mommy is very hurried and adjusted their prediction accordingly. ("Mommy is in a hurry, so this time it will be a super-short visit, and we won't have dessert.") Otto is angry, not because he has to miss out on something he likes, but because the "script" in his head for visiting a hamburger restaurant is off. His script is absolute: hamburger + fries + soft drink + ice cream.

Perhaps there are also a few details in his script that children without autism do not have in their script, such as the specific place where he will sit in the restaurant, what the box with the hamburger says, the brand of the soft drink. Otto's predictions are absolute and very precise. A brain that predicts that way faces many more unpleasant surprises. It suffers from changes that other children suffer much less from because they already saw them coming from context.

During the sports day at school, Max gets bored during the breaks. Unlike during a normal school day, Max is not so sure what he can do during the breaks. He is a little out of his usual routine. The teacher notices this and suggests playing a game of basketball with him. Max loves basketball, and his teacher knows it. When Max scores a goal, the teacher shouts, "Wow! Good job, Max!" Max looks at the teacher angrily and says, "You can't say that! You're not allowed to say that at all!" The teacher doesn't get it. He thinks it's right to give kids kudos when they score. But Max is confused by the compliment, and the world no longer makes sense to him. His brain has an absolute idea of cheering: you only support your own team. The teacher here violates that absolute rule by also supporting Max, the opposing team. In Max's thinking, that is not possible.

Rob received emotion-recognition training at school as a toddler. He was shown pictures of facial expressions and learned to name them with the words angry, scared, happy, sad.

With the picture about grief, the therapist had pointed out tears. When Rob watched a medal ceremony at the Olympics and saw an athlete shed a tear when she was awarded the silver medal, he no longer understood. Surely she should be happy? In Rob's brain, there is an absolute link between tears and sadness. That there are also tears of happiness is confusing to a brain that thinks absolutely.

In their behavior, children with autism can differ greatly from one another, but what they all have in common is absolute thinking. Their ideas about the world are straightforward (something can only mean one thing), precise, and detailed, while the world is very relative. Eating an ice cream, cheering, and facial expressions can take on interpretations that are constantly different. This leads to a lot of confusion, frustration, misunderstanding, stress, and anxiety in autistic brains.

Millie panics when the teacher tells the children in class that tomorrow Rosie is "going to the ocean with Daddy." Millie shouts out loud, "No!" The teacher confirms that Rosie is indeed going to the ocean with Daddy. Millie shouts even louder, "No!" Only later, when her mom hears the story of the panic attack, does everything become clear: to Millie's brain, "Daddy" is her daddy. Why would her daddy suddenly go to the ocean with another child?

This "absolute thinking" cannot be changed.

This typical autistic style of predicting the world is lifelong.

Thus, autism cannot be cured or solved. Children with autism can learn a lot so that there is less misunderstanding, stress, or confusion, but there will always be a difference from other children. When a child with autism exhibits a challenging behavior (such as a tantrum or refusing something), it is important to look beyond the behavior and look for the invisible, absolute thinking that is causing that behavior. As a parent or teacher, you can then better deal with that behavior. If you know that Millie's "no!" does not mean that she does not want another child to go to the ocean with her daddy but occurs out of confusion and fear, then you deal with that "no" in a very different way. You no longer see it as a protest, but as a protection against fear and confusion. What Millie needs is not a call to grant other children a trip to the ocean with their father, but an explanation that pushes the context button: "Every child has a daddy, and Rosie is going to the ocean with her daddy, not your daddy."

A world without absolute rules (sometimes there is an ice cream, sometimes not; a tear is sometimes sadness, sometimes something else; sometimes someone supports the opposing team) is a world full of uncertainty, a world with many ambiguities, and especially a very unpredictable world. (How do you know if there will be an ice cream or not?) That is at the heart of autism: uncertainty.

If a child with autism exhibits difficult behavior, it is important to look beyond the behavior and look for the invisible.

ADDITIONAL FEATURES

The typical thinking style of the autistic brain leads not only to the already mentioned behavioral characteristics of autism (difficulty in social contact, in communication, and in response to the environment), but also to other characteristics that we often see in children with autism:

- **Difficulties coping with (especially unpredictable) stimuli**, such as sound, touch, light, certain clothes, or fabrics: if you can't properly anticipate what your senses will have to process, these stimuli quickly create sensory overload.
- **Eating problems:** absolute thinking about food can lead to refusal of certain foods. For example, yogurt has no chunks, a carrot is sliced only one way, vegetables must be green.
- **Sleep problems** arise due to confusion, frustration, misunderstandings, stress, and anxiety.
- Nothing has a fixed meaning, not even one's own bodily signals. **This also causes children with autism to have difficulty reading their own bodies.** This can lead to potty training problems as well as difficulties with emotion regulation.
- Because **they do not always understand the world well** and see that other children apparently have much less trouble with it, some children with autism develop negative ideas about themselves. They consider themselves

stupid or less worthy. They also have more frequent experiences of failure.

- In some cases, this may even result in a **loss of motivation** to learn: "Why should I try? I won't succeed anyway."
- Because these children **suffer more stress**, autism can also lead to depression or additional anxiety problems.

Apart from these problems, of course, children with autism also have many nice and beautiful qualities. These come to the surface especially in an environment where they are comfortable, and where attention is paid not only to the difficulties but also to the positives. Absolute thinking and a sense of precision make children with autism excel at certain things, such as remembering dates and facts, noticing details, and strictly following rules. They often have an incredibly strong sense of justice. Because they think differently, they often come up with unusual and creative solutions. And they sometimes know a lot about certain topics. If you try to highlight these traits in particular, you help both the child and yourself to look more acceptingly at moments when things are difficult. You'll read more about that later in this book.

... children with autism also have many nice and beautiful qualities. These come to the surface especially in an environment where they are comfortable, and where attention is paid not only to the difficulties but also to the positives.

WHAT IS AUTISM NOT?

The characteristics of autism overlap to some extent with those of other diagnoses. In practice, it is not easy to distinguish autism from other developmental conditions and disabilities. Nevertheless, autism differs from the following diagnoses, among others:

- **Intellectual disability.** Many children with developmental delays exhibit autistic behavior to a greater or lesser extent. In some children with autism, the developmental delay is initially more noticeable than the autism. The developmental level of social skills and social imagination in autistic children is always noticeably lower than their general level of development. In children with intellectual disabilities without autism, this difference is not so great.
- **ADHD.** Children with autism can be very busy and hyperactive, especially at preschool age. Conversely, quite a few children with ADHD have social-emotional difficulties. But the overlapping characteristics have a different background: with ADHD, impulsivity and concentration problems are the main cause; with autism, the children do not understand the world or understand it differently.
- **Language and speech development disorders.** Although a language development delay is not uncommon in children with autism, it is not a specific characteristic. It is primarily a consequence of the general developmental delay that some children with autism have and of the problems with understanding communication in general.

- **Reactive attachment disorder.** This disorder is characterized by pronounced contact issues, which can also occur in children with autism, for example, extreme familiarity with strangers, not wanting to be comforted, rejecting contact, or indifference. But the contact problems in an attachment disorder result from the child's neglect or mistreatment, and not from an innate difficulty in forming relationships.
- **Hypersensitivity and over-stimulation.** Our world is becoming busier and more complex, so children become more over-stimulated. As a result of this over-stimulation, they exhibit behaviors very similar to autism.
- **Over-stimulation** is usually a result of stress and a brain that is hyperalert. Autistic brains are no more or less sensitive to stimuli than others, but because they struggle more with uncertainty, children with autism are also easily overstimulated. Hypersensitive people are often also very sensitive to social stimuli and to what others are thinking and feeling, but with autism, figuring out and inferring thoughts and emotions are a difficulty.
- **Obsessive-compulsive disorder.** This disorder is characterized by (unrealistic) compulsive thoughts, such as a fear of tainting, and by compulsive actions, such as extreme cleaning or continuous hand washing. Being absorbed by certain ideas or themes, expressing resistance to change, and stubbornly sticking to certain habits and rituals in the case of autism may be reminiscent of obsessive-compulsive disorder. But again, the

background of the behavior is different. Children with autism are usually not aware of the compulsive nature of their behavior or thoughts, nor are they usually bothered by it.

- **Tics and Tourette's syndrome.** Tourette's syndrome manifests itself through involuntary movements (such as suddenly extending an arm or a leg or making jumps) and through vocal tics (the reproduction of certain sounds, such as clearing one's throat or making sounds, hissing, and/or pronouncing certain words involuntarily, rather than often cursing or swearing). The stereotyped behaviors of people with autism can be confused with tics. The differentiation between tics and repeated movements is not always easy, but tics are more likely to be involuntary, while repeated stereotyped movements of children with autism are more deliberate.
- **Dyspraxia.** Dyspraxia or developmental coordination disorder (DCD) is a disorder in the coordination of movements, the performance of actions and the learning and automatization of motor skills. Children with autism often also have problems with the execution of actions, but in their case, it is not so much a motor coordination problem but rather the consequence of not being able to plan an action, not knowing how to perform something, and not being able to switch from one partial act to another. Some children with autism move woodenly and are also clumsy, but other children with autism are just more motor agile than age-matched peers, at least during their favorite activity.

- **Oppositional-defiant behavior disorder.** Children with this disorder exhibit negativistic, hostile, defiant, and overtly disobedient behavior toward adults, especially parents and other educators. Although children with autism can also be rebellious and disobedient at times, it will usually not be directed at the parents as individuals. Rather, they are rebellious against changes or because they did not understand the assignment properly.
- **Social anxiety disorder/social phobia.** A social phobia is an extreme fear or extreme discomfort in everyday social situations. The child is afraid of being watched, blushing, being criticized, or doing or saying the wrong thing. As a result, the child avoids all kinds of social situations. Children with autism, because they do not understand social interaction well, may also fear and avoid certain social situations, but the cause of their fear is that they are at the mercy of the overly complex and incomprehensible social world. With a phobia, there is the realization that the fear is extreme and unfounded, but the child cannot suppress the fear.

Distinguishing all these disorders from each other and from autism requires expertise on the part of the diagnostician. By the way, autism can coexist with any of these disorders and impairments and sometimes even with several of them. It requires a comprehensive examination and therefore a lot of time. This can lengthen the duration of the diagnostic process. This is frustrating, especially if, in the meantime, you want to get started and guide the child well.

NEEDS AND STRATEGIES

The autistic way of perceiving and understanding the world is not the only thing that shapes the behavior of children with autism. Behind every behavior is also a need. So try to look through children's behavior and find out the need(s) behind the behavior. Then together you can find strategies to meet those specific need(s) in a more appropriate way. A child having a tantrum because he is overexcited needs different solutions than a child frustrated by a lack of participation.

Children's needs are universal. That means they apply to every child. But children with autism might require a specific approach. The needs you read about in this book are based on self-determination theory, a well-researched model of growth and functioning. This theory states that every human being needs three important "vitamins for growth": autonomy, connectedness, and competence. This is no different for a child with autism. But translating these three needs to the classroom or home situation requires an approach that takes into account the possibilities and difficulties that may crop up in an autistic brain.

So try to look through children's behavior and find out the need(s) behind the behavior. Then together you can find strategies to meet those specific need(s) in a more appropriate way.

This autism-friendly approach is characterized by the need to be genuinely understood and receive clarity and predictability. That's why you'll find these three needs first in this book. They are the foundations of an autism-friendly home or school environment. All other needs rely on them. Children without autism also need clarity and predictability, but children with autism depend heavily on adults and an appropriate environment to achieve this. Other children can often meet those needs for themselves.

Following these three needs, you will read how to fill in the "vitamins for growth" in different ways for the child with autism, matching the child's unique way of thinking.

Children with autism have ten major needs:

1. Being understood
2. Clarity
3. Predictability
4. Autonomy
5. Connection
6. Good agreements and rules
7. Positive self-esteem
8. Contentment
9. Meaning
10. Encouragement

In what follows, you will find out exactly what these needs of children with autism are. You will get strategies with concrete tips on how to meet these needs more fully. For the well-being of children with autism, it is important that you give them what they really need. By providing a needs-supportive environment both at home and in the classroom, you can avoid a lot of stress and behavioral difficulties.

By providing a needs-supportive environment both at home and in the classroom, you can avoid a lot of stress and behavioral difficulties.

1

BEING UNDERSTOOD

"A child who perceives and thinks differently will respond differently to the world."

BEING UNDERSTOOD
WHAT IS IT?

As a parent or teacher, you want to help children with autism grow up to become the best version of themselves, strengthened in life against all possible challenges they will encounter on their path. This includes messages that make clear what is possible and what is not, what the norm is, and what is considered inappropriate. Every child, whether autistic or not, learns from the boundaries you set as a parent or teacher. Not everything the child says or does is automatically okay.

When helping children with autism grow up, a view beyond labels and behaviors is fundamental. Challenging behavior of autistic children is often not about not wanting something, but about not (yet) being able to do something. Children without autism pick up certain norms and rules spontaneously and intuitively; in children with autism, this process is more difficult. They often need much more clarity and predictability. Not taking into account what is really going on in their heads will lead to even more frustration and stress and, consequently, to even more escalating behavior such as contradicting, tantrums, and disobedience. This way you end up in a vicious circle: you don't understand the child, and the child doesn't understand you. In the long run, the child then feels more and more different and alone.

Keep in mind that the child has a developmental condition. Don't expect that the behavior will disappear on its own, or that the child will just have to make more effort to adapt to all kinds of norms and expectations. Children with autism can learn a lot about expected behaviors and are often very motivated to do so, but that doesn't always happen by itself. Your support helps tremendously, as long as it also starts from a need and not from a negative view of the behavior.

Focus on what is going well rather than on negative behavior. This helps the child, and you, to persevere.

This is certainly not always easy. You will often wonder why the child sometimes does or does not do something, or why he or she exhibits behavior that you do not immediately know where it comes from. Remember that it comes from somewhere and has a cause in autistic thinking. A good conversation with the network of the child, your partner, or your colleague can sometimes take a totally different look at the behavior. Also, focusing on what is going well rather than on negative behavior helps both the child and yourself to persevere when things are difficult.

But don't look at every behavior from the angle of autism either. Children with autism are also just children. And they sometimes do things that adults find annoying. Children sometimes get angry or make mistakes. They sometimes don't listen to their parents or don't feel like doing homework. You don't have to keep looking at that as behavior exclusively resulting from autistic thinking.

In essence, children with autism want to be understood. As a child. With autism. So that their environment does not view them as a "bad" child. So that you can offer them help that matches their needs. That way you can make a difference for these beautiful children that you want to make stronger in life.

Tim has a hard time staying at the table during breakfast. He takes a bite and then gets up again. Sometimes he comes back quickly for another bite, but sometimes it takes as much as five minutes before he gets back to his chair. Consequently, each meal easily takes an hour, forcing me to run every day and often arrive late to work. This scene causes a lot of stress in our family life. Remarks like, "Stay in your chair during breakfast!" have no effect at all. Tim's behavior doesn't change.

JONAS, DAD OF TIM, NINE YEARS OLD

During math lessons, classroom practice moments are alternated with individual exercises. I notice that Myra follows very attentively during the classroom practice moment. She sits up straight and looks at the board while I explain. But when I ask her to continue practicing the material independently, Myra does nothing. She keeps staring at me, and each time I have to repeat, "Start your exercise, Myra." And then she seems to wake up. For a moment. A few moments later Myra stares at the board again and doesn't fill in anything.

CAROLINE, TEACHER OF MYRA, ELEVEN YEARS OLD

HOW CAN YOU SUPPORT THIS NEED?

STRATEGY 1: Look beyond behavior

The behavior of children with autism can be compared to an iceberg: you only see a piece of it and not even the main part or the essence that is hidden under the water. So if you are confronted with behavior of children with autism that can be troublesome, put on your goggles and look underwater at the cause of that behavior. If you don't, you stay above water, focused on the behavior. You try to eliminate pieces of the negative behavior with responses such as punishment. But you know yourself what happens when you chop away pieces of a visible iceberg: the iceberg will rebalance, and that means the same or sometimes more or different negative behavior will surface.

Looking beyond the behavior means looking for the cause of that behavior, without quick interpretations. Calling a child who puts his head on the school desk "unmotivated" is an interpretation of behavior, but is it the only one? And is it the right one? Perhaps by doing this the child is just trying to focus properly on what you are saying.

- **Don't just address behavior.** Behavior is often a reaction to uncertainty in the brain. Try to understand the child by thinking about what causes doubt, fear, or stress. Dare to question the child about this, but do so only when they have calmed down. Children with autism have a hard time articulating exactly what is bothering them under stress.

- **Think preventively to avoid challenging behavior.** Engage with the child and ask what is still unclear.

  HOME: *Before the family outing, ask your child if they still have ambiguities, questions or fears.*

  SCHOOL: *Make time during your lesson to ask briefly if the child has understood everything correctly. Don't wait until the end of the lesson to do this. Sometimes the stress is too much by then.*

- **Don't take challenging behavior personally.** Behavior is often directed toward an unclear situation rather than people. For example, if the child calls you a stupid teacher, it does not necessarily mean that they think you are stupid, but rather that they do not like the situation they are in.

- **Consider difficult behavior as a request for help.** The child is stuck in frustration but cannot always express it in an appropriate way.

  HOME: *In moments of stress, don't overwhelm your child with all kinds of questions, such as, "What's going on?" or, "What's the problem?" Answering those questions is sometimes very difficult when the stress is too high. Therefore, ask these questions only when your child has calmed down.*

  SCHOOL: *Make asking for help easy. For example, a card on the table that the child can turn to indicate they want to ask a question. This is easier for children with autism than raising their hand.*

- **Limit your responses that don't look underwater.** Punishing a child only for what they did wrong or rewarding them indiscriminately for what goes right does not always help in the long term. Sure you may or even should make it clear what the child did wrong or right, but always start from what the child has not understood well, and try to clarify this for the child.

- **Don't be too quick to think, "I don't see a problem, so there's no problem."** Many children with autism camouflage or mask their stress or panic and "explode" into another situation where it seems safer to them. Therefore, check regularly at a set time how the child is doing, so that they sense that it is safe to give an honest answer. Make this a regular ritual so that you don't forget to ask.

- **View yourself as a source of security or confidence** if you are often confronted with challenging behavior.

STRATEGY 2: Be open to an alternative approach

Looking beneath the surface for the cause of behavior is not always easy. Many children with autism are not so fluent in expressing where their stress comes from or what is unclear to them. This is certainly true if the stress has already overtaken them. Few children in such a situation can express what is going on and what they need to calm down in a relaxed, polite way.

In addition, certain behaviors can have many different causes (and therefore solutions). For example, a child who does not cooperate in class may show that behavior because something is unclear, but equally so because they do not find the subject meaningful or do not know how to start the task. There may even be a sensory cause underlying behavior that looks like a lack of cooperation.

In such a case, it is sometimes more interesting to see how the child functions in a different environment. Do you see little cooperation for a particular school subject? Then explore how things are going outside the walls of your classroom: with colleagues in other classes, or even beyond the school. How are things going at home? With the hobby or sports club? Maybe there is an approach outside your own walls that seems to work better with the child. If parents and teachers are open to mutual tips and feedback, it is always to the benefit of the child with autism.

- **Don't be immediately discouraged if your help doesn't seem to be working.** Try to look beyond one unique cause of the behavior.

- **Engage with other educators of the child with autism.** What interpretation do they give to certain behaviors? A different perspective sometimes brings new, fresh interpretations and ideas.

- **Do not interpret a request for help from another person as a sign of weakness.** When parents seek advice from teachers or the other way around, it is just a sign that they want the best for the child.

- **Do you have tips or helpful advice for another person?** Then don't shout them as commands over the wall of your home or school. That's how neighborly quarrels start. As an adult, listen to other's needs and help where you can.

- **Everyone likes predictable routines.** Agree on a regular consultation time with other educators to evaluate the approach chosen and the progress made.

- **Schedule an informal consultation** as soon as you feel the need. Don't wait until certain behaviors escalate too far.

STRATEGY 3: Focus on moments when things are going well

As educators engage in conversations with each other to better understand children with autism, there is an important rule: Do not talk too much, and certainly not only about the difficulties you are experiencing at home or at school. Of course, it can be relieving to vent to each other and to hear that in another context there are also peaks and valleys, that some things go well and at other times things are difficult.

But you may well end up in a problem spiral as a result. "What gets attention, grows," says a solution-focused slogan. If you give (too) much attention to problems and difficult moments, you see more and more of them. Sometimes educators then start pointing fingers at each other as the cause of the challenging behavior.

Even when talking to the child himself, it does not always make much sense to analyze difficult moments or discuss challenging behavior. Ignoring difficulties is also a behavioral response, and that usually doesn't do you much good either. In many situations, it is good to try to figure out exactly what is difficult, unclear, or stressful by comparing it to moments when things are going just fine. Focus on those moments of success, progress, and growth rather than problem situations if you want to understand a child with autism. It can be very instructive to look inside or outside your own context for activities, people, places, or moments where the child is calm, happy, or functioning well. Look at such situations as a source of inspiration. Why does the child behave differently there? What are you doing differently? What helps the child there? What calms the child? And following that: how can you do much more of that in the current context?

- **Always start conversations with other educators with positive situations,** moments when everything is going smoothly: tell each other what is going well, what progress has been made, and what kind of support is working well.

- **Do the same in a conversation with the child with autism at home or in the classroom.** Compliment the child on all those positive moments.

- **Try to identify what makes those moments so good:** what is so different in terms of clarity, support, presence of others, sensory stimuli, time of day.

- **Think about how you can use the elements from successful moments** much more, inside and outside your own context.

2

CLARITY

‘Clarity brings peace to a brain that is full of doubts.’

CLARITY
WHAT IS IT?

Children with autism find it difficult to understand the intentions behind words or pictures and decipher the meanings of stimuli spontaneously. Their brain thinks absolutely, with fixed meanings. For example, they may think like this: “If someone smiles at me, he thinks I am funny,” “If someone yells, he is angry,” “If there is nothing in my calendar, I don’t have to do anything.” However, some people laugh when they are very nervous. Those who shout are sometimes not angry but only very enthusiastic. And “Studying your lessons” is not always noted in the agenda but simply expected.

Communication and all that it entails is difficult for children with autism. An assignment in a school calendar, a verbal explanation to a game, a pictogram on a daily schedule, a look from the teacher, all of these are communication: they convey a message intentionally or unintentionally. But your words, body language, pictograms, or pictures can have quite a few meanings. Those are dependent on context. Children with autism do not spontaneously use that context to retrieve meanings, intentions, or expectations. As a result, it is sometimes difficult for them to understand what you want to say or what exactly is expected of them.

Communication connects people with and without autism. But communication in our world is full of unspoken, vague, or double meanings. For people with autism, nothing is self-explanatory. It helps them when you make the expectations and intentions visible. You can do that by writing things down in words, using pictures, or showing objects. This ensures that less doubt arises. Yet visual communication is not automatically clear. After all, nothing has just one fixed meaning. Therefore, communication should above all be clear for children with autism.

For people with autism, nothing is obvious. Make expectations and intentions visible by, for example, showing pictures or objects.

For people with autism, nothing is obvious. Make expectations and intentions visible by, for example, showing pictures or objects.

You often think the content or intent of a message is clear, but is that really true? It is certainly not always easy to look at your own verbal or nonverbal communication from a different perspective. And if you then find that a child with autism is not doing what you expected or were trying to achieve with your message, you may be quick to place the blame on the child. Dare to be self-critical and check if your communication was clear.

"I've told Maria a hundred times not to just throw her coat on the floor, but she just keeps doing it! She just won't listen!"

Is it clear to Maria where the coat does belong? And how was this made clear to her? Apparently she has been told a hundred times what not to do, but was there an alternative? And if saying something turns out not to work, can it be done in another way? Maria's behavior may have nothing at all to do with "not wanting to listen." Does Maria even understand the message?

Offer clarity about what is meant or expected. This gives more certainty to a child with autism and brings many benefits. First and foremost, clarity brings more peace to a brain that is full of doubts. In addition, clear communication can help the child function more independently.

After all, they don't have to ask you all the time to explain exactly what you meant.

Of course, there is one important prerequisite: offer the clarity in an autism-friendly way, both what you communicate (the content) and how you do it (the form).

You may now be thinking to yourself, "Oh, but I am clear in my messages, because I give lots of explanations!" or, "I visualize tasks with pictures. That's autism-friendly, isn't it?" Unfortunately, autism-friendly communication is not a checklist. As with anything to do with autism, it needs to be tailor-made. Just because you explain a lot or make something visual doesn't mean it's is also clear to a child with autism. It is a true art to adapt your communication to the need for clarity. But if you observe the following strategies, you are already on the right track.

Autism-friendly communication is unfortunately not a checklist; it is customized.

Ellen always asks me what she's going to have for dinner tonight. When I answer "French fries!" she laughs. She does this every time she hears those words, but I also hear her asking for more clarity and certainty: "I can't speak French, but that doesn't matter, because one shouldn't talk with food in ones mouth, right?

CARLA, MOM OF ELLEN, AGE SEVEN

Tom's calendar said, "Geometry test: the triangle." We noticed that this caused him a lot of stress. It was not so much that the test itself was difficult for Tom, but understanding what exactly he was supposed to be learning. Calculating areas? Drawing triangles? It wasn't clear to him. Because of this uncertainty, Tom then just memorized everything about the triangle in his textbook. He could recite every exercise, every drawing, every page number on the test.

RICHARD, SIXTH GRADE TEACHER

coat on the coat rack
shoes on the shelf
close the door

HOW CAN YOU SUPPORT THIS NEED?

STRATEGY 1: Communicate unambiguously

Children with autism have a hard time when the meaning of a message is not immediately clear from the context. For example, if a pictogram shows only a ball, the message can go quite a few ways. "Is it playtime then? Are we going to play soccer or volleyball? Or can I play by myself? And does it have to be a ball game? With that exact ball?" Maybe as a teacher you just want to show a nice picture. If you want to make your message autism-friendly, it should also say specifically what it means: unambiguous communication makes what you mean and expect clear.

- **Say exactly what you mean.** Then children with autism won't have to interpret your communication.

  HOME: *If you use a picture of a plate with cutlery in a daily schedule to make a meal time predictable, clarify to your child that a meal time can also consist of sandwiches where you do not use cutlery.*

  SCHOOL: *"When you think you are done, you may stop," is more difficult to interpret than, "When you have completed all the exercises, turn in your sheet."*

- **Use short sentences, but don't be terse.** Being more to the point often means less stress for children with autism. "Would you give me the water please?" is still polite if you make it, "Give me the water please?"

- **Address the child with autism personally.** This makes it easier for him to understand that the (group) instruction also applies to him .

- **Clarify vague words by making them contextual.**

  HOME: *"Soon Grandpa and Grandma will come," is more vague than, "Grandma and Grandpa will come after dinner."*

  SCHOOL: Learning *is a word with many meanings. Clarify for the child with autism what you mean by learning, depending on the context: practicing, rereading, memorizing.*

- **Give one message at a time.** Ask one question at a time. Give one assignment at a time. So for a sentence like, "How was your weekend, and did you meet up with your boyfriend yet?" it's best to make two questions.

- **Do you expect the child with autism to do something? Then make that clear as well.** The child cannot always infer that from the context.

- **Adapt your language to the age and intelligence of the child.** Normally gifted teens can use clarity, not kindergarten talk.

- **Are you joking? Then say so.** Irony, metaphors, or sayings are not always clear from the context.

- Also "subtitle" your own behavior. **Say what you are going to do and why you are doing it.** That predictability gives children with autism peace of mind.

  HOME: *"At the party I'm going to say hello to everyone so people know we're here. After that, I'll come back and sit next to you."*

  SCHOOL: *"I'll stop by after five minutes to see if everything works out with the exercise. Then you can ask me for help."*

- **Check how the child understood your message or instruction.** To do so, avoid asking, "Do you understand?" or, "Do you understand everything?" and ask action questions such as, "What did you remember from the explanation?", "What are you going to do next?" and, "What did you find difficult?" Also, give an explanation or demonstration a second time if necessary. Don't expect everything to be immediately clear.

STRATEGY 2: Use positive messages

If you want to help children with autism with difficult situations at school or at home, it is best not to take "wrong" behavior, such as something going wrong, not working very well (yet), or being inappropriate, as a starting point. Clarifying that something was "rude" or "wrong" does not exactly help these children, as we talked about earlier. That's because the sometimes logical, correct alternative is not at all obvious to an autistic brain.

You undoubtedly know the psychological trick: "Don't think of a pink elephant." Whether you like it or not, that pink elephant flashes through your mind for a moment, because it is explicitly mentioned in the instruction. Coming up with an alternative is not so easy for children with autism. And then that pink elephant lingers much longer. Therefore, clarity consists of as many positive messages as possible: just say what you expect instead of what you don't expect.

- **Give positively worded instructions that make it clear what the child should do** rather than what he or she should not do.

  HOME: *"No running in the house," is better said as, "Walk quietly in the house." Or "Don't eat with your hands," is better said as, "Eat with your knife and fork."*

  SCHOOL: *"Don't interrupt each other," is better said as, "Let each other speak." Or "Don't use a calculator," is better replaced by, "Add this in your head."*

- Also, all kinds of images, such as pictures, drawings or pictograms, sometimes show what is not possible or allowed, with a cross or red line through it. **Rather, use images that show what is possible and allowed.**

- **Use the same positive wording** when it comes to where a child may go, when they can do something, with whom they can do it, how they are supposed to carry out an activity, etc.

- Good examples generate good ideas. **Let them see you doing something** without going into too much detail about what is wrong.

STRATEGY 3: Visualize your message

Formulating the content of your message, explanation, or instruction unambiguously and positively brings clarity to children with autism. But the packaging, the form, is equally important. Verbal language is perhaps the most widely used form of communication, but it is only useful if both parties understand each other. While on vacation abroad, you have probably encountered the limitations of spoken language yourself. Furthermore, spoken language is sometimes difficult because it disappears as quickly as it is spoken. Visible forms of communication are often clearer. They also "stick" longer, giving a child with autism more time to figure out and process their meaning. A choice between different visible forms of communication always comes down to: which form does the child understand best?

- **So choose a form of communication that suits the specific child.** Not all children who can read, understand written language most easily. Not all children find pictograms clear.

  – **Use objects to show what you mean.**

  HOME: *On purpose, always leave one pair of socks in the dresser drawer. This makes it clear to your child where to put the other socks when they want to help put away laundry.*

  SCHOOL: *Put a basket on your desk that makes it clear where the children should put their tasks when they are done.*

- **Images can make things clear.** This can include pictograms, drawings, and pictures (listed from least clear to clearest, respectively).

HOME: *You can put a picture of socks on the sock drawer.*

SCHOOL: *Hang a pictogram on your desk to make it clear where the children should put the tasks.*

- **Written language is still useful visual information, but already a lot more abstract.** You can use it only if the child can understand what he or she is reading.

HOME: *On the sock drawer, you can set up the word "socks" visibly.*

SCHOOL: *Put a note or paper on your desk saying, "Turn in your task here."*

- **Gestures or body language are also visible, but that form of communication does not remain visual as long as the preceding forms.** However, supporting your verbal language with it is certainly not a bad idea.

HOME: *Smile at your child when they helped you put away the laundry while saying, "This makes me happy."*

SCHOOL: *Point to the basket where a task should be placed to make clear exactly which basket you mean while saying, "Put your task in the basket."*

○ **Don't visualize every word you say.** Focus on important information that the child definitely needs to know or remember.

- **Use outlines, roadmaps, and drawings.** You can use them in a variety of ways to bring more clarity and predictability.

  HOME: *Hang the weekend schedule of the various family members in a visible place. This brings clarity to all family members, not just your child with autism.*

  SCHOOL: *Write the lesson structure on the whiteboard and check off a section each time it is finished.*

- **Also use diagrams, arrows, lines, or colors to convey your message clearly.** Make it clear exactly what you mean by those diagrams, arrows, lines, and colors.

- **Do not overdo it with text or images.** Excess does harm when it comes to children with autism, because they can easily encounter information overload.

- **Make sure your visible communication is available** so the child can refer to it again if needed.

- **Remember that visible communication is clear only when it is also unambiguously and positively worded.**

3

PREDICTABILITY

'At times with little certainty, predictability gives us a grip.'

PREDICTABILITY
WHAT IS IT?

Children with autism have difficulties predicting what will happen to them. This often requires some form of imagination. They have to imagine a lot of things they may never have experienced before. Sometimes these things lie in the future, and it is certainly impossible to predict them with certainty. Without an overview, the minds of those with autism are full of chaos.

It also sometimes happens that children with autism get lost, literally and figuratively. They may not have completed all the assignments you offered. Toys have disappeared at home that should have been in the right place. Homework assignments are submitted late or not at all. These are all possible signs that the child misses predictability and an overview of what is to be expected.

Children's home or school environments are full of stimuli that are not easy for a brain with autism to predict. Being autism-friendly means making those stimuli predictable and clear through the clear communication. (You can read about in the previous chapter on the need for clarity.) This allows children with autism to survive in the chaotic environment first and foremost, and also to be motivated to engage in all kinds of activities in the home or school environment.

This environment can be interpreted broadly: it is not only the physical space; it is also all the stimuli that the brain receives. Some of these stimuli are offered deliberately. Think of tasks at school, activities on the weekend, or material in leisure time.

What a child with autism needs in terms of predictability is person- and context-specific. So always start with the unique child.

Other stimuli may be more simply present, with no specific intention, such as noises on the street, siblings at the table, or materials you don't need for an activity.

These stimuli are all part of the environment, and the brain has to "do something" with all of them: process them by attaching much or little meaning to them. But that is contextual: it depends on the situation whether the child should pay much or little attention to the brother at the table, for example. During a table game they should pay attention to him, if the game involves turn taking. During homework, probably not, because homework is rather individual. This contextual sensitivity is particularly difficult for children with autism, which is why it is important to bring predictability into the classroom or home environment.

So, what do you have to make clear and predictable, at home or in the classroom, to give these children a little more peace of mind? The answer is simpler than the application: anything that is not clear and predictable. Of course, this is very person- and context-specific. So always start with what a unique child with autism needs in terms of predictability.

Erik likes to play in the garden. But since the neighbors got a dog, things have changed. Because of the wall that separates our garden from the neighbors, Erik can't see the dog. Sometimes the animal suddenly starts barking when Erik is playing in the yard, although you are never sure if and when that will happen. That uncertainty creates a lot of anxiety. By clarifying for Erik every time he goes outside to play that the neighbor's dog might bark, we offer him predictability. It doesn't make the turmoil disappear completely, but for Erik it becomes manageable.

JOHN, DAD OF ERIK, TWELVE YEARS OLD

Nicolas has a lot of stress before every school trip. Not letting him go on the trip would remove that stress, but both Nicolas and his parents, teachers and fellow students find that quite unfortunate. With a clear program of activities during the school outing, we give Nicolas more predictability, and peace returns.

CHRIS, FIFTH GRADE TEACHER

help you choose
a book
listen when
you're
having a
hard time
help
with
tasks
buddy

HOW CAN YOU SUPPORT THIS NEED?

STRATEGY 1: Make PLATO predictable

An autistic brain finds it hard to predict the world, which creates a lot of uncertainty. Sometimes an autistic brain also makes too-specific predictions that do not match reality, and these cause a lot of stress. For example, a child may sometimes think that french fries will be eaten on every outing because it happened once, or that every zoo has panda bears just like the ones he has seen on television.

To create clear and comforting predictability, you can use the PLATO principles. PLATO is an acronym that helps you remember what children with autism sometimes have difficulty figuring out spontaneously and intuitively:

People
Location
Activity
Time
Organization

PEOPLE. People are perhaps one of the most unpredictable stimuli in the environment of someone with autism. Sometimes they are there, sometimes they are not. Sometimes they are there but you don't see them. Sometimes there are an awful lot of them, but no one you are looking for. An overview is in order then:

- **Make it clear who will attend activities.**

  HOME: *Set up a visible list of who is coming to a family party, or make it visually clear on a weekly chart who is bringing your child to school and picking them up.*

  SCHOOL: *Use a system with pictures to immediately make it visually clear which teacher will be present.*

- **Clarify the different roles of individuals:** who can the child go to with questions, or who can the child go to with which question?

- **A buddy system can be very helpful.** Pair a child with autism with a peer in the classroom or sports club. This way it is quickly clear who the child can ask for help.

- **Clearly agree when and how a buddy may be called in for any questions and/or emergencies.**

LOCATION. You can also make clear and predictable different places where an activity will take place and possibly the materials the child with autism will need in the activity.

- **Clarify with autism-friendly communication where a child with autism should be or what they can find where.** Plotted routes, maps, layouts of cupboards, contents of boxes—you can make it all clear.

- **Also consider some important places, such as the reception area, restrooms, and dining areas.**

- **Make it clear where a child can find a quiet place or where they can go if they can't handle the situation anymore.**

  HOME: *Agree with your child that they can go to the bedroom if the house gets too crowded.*

  SCHOOL: *Make it clear where the child with autism can find peace and quiet when things don't go well on the playground.*

- **If the same location is used for different purposes, clarify these functions** (e.g., as a school canteen, recreation room, fitness room, movie theater, etc.).

- **Give a tour or demonstration at new places or with new materials or situations**, even if they seem "the same" to you. Autistic brains notice (even small) differences more than similarities.

ACTIVITIES. Predictability can also focus more on exactly what the child with autism will be doing: a clear task overview, a class schedule, the planned training exercises, the program of an outing.

- **Create a schedule or program in which you make predictable what the child will do** (or by extension all children in the class or family) and what is expected of the child then.

- **Also include "logical" activities that may not be so obvious to a child with autism in your planning:** "After soccer practice, we go home," "After play, you have to clean up," etc.

- **Use a tick-box system in your visual overview of activities.** This allows a child with autism to clearly track what has already passed and what is yet to come.

- **Provide a small transition moment between an arrival or break and an activity,** for example. This allows children with autism to acclimate for a while.

- **Also provide fun, relaxing, calming activities in the program.** That way, a child knows when he or she can take a moment to discharge or just recharge for "unpleasant" or stressful activities.

TIMES (DURATION). Activities take place at a specific time. Sometimes it is important to clarify that moment and to make predictable how long an activity will last.

- **Provide an overview of when something is due.** Daily or weekly schedules, diaries, planners, etc. are useful for the whole class or family.

- **Stick to your schedule.** For example, if you are not sure you will be able to go to the supermarket at 4:00 PM, then it is better not to use an exact time. Instead say, for instance, "We will go after the afternoon snack."

- **Different types of timers, hourglasses, and color clocks can make the time duration of activities visible and predictable.**

- **Briefly announce the end of a break or the beginning of an activity in advance.** This makes your intentions and expectations more predictable.

ORGANIZATION. For a lot of activities, it is not only necessary to clarify what you expect from a child, but also to make predictable exactly how to go about it.

- **Roadmaps tailored to the competencies of a child with autism make it clear how to do a task or activity.**
- **Is a particular order necessary?** Then clarify that with clear communication.
- **Do you expect a certain behavior in the process?** Then make that predictable and clear with unambiguous and positively worded communication.

  HOME: *Do you expect your child to stay at the table at restaurants? If so, make that predictable in advance and offer the child an activity to engage in at the table.*

  SCHOOL: *Do you want exercises to be done in silence? Then clarify that at the start and make sure every child follows through.*

STRATEGY 2: Focus on what is lasting

Of course, it is impossible to make everything predictable. Sometimes you yourself don't know exactly what is going to happen, who will be present or how long something will take. Other times you think you have a perfect schedule ready but an unexpected change pops up and the program is all messed up.

Changes are often very frightening for children with autism whose brains are looking for certainties. For many children, doubt sets in: What will change? What are the consequences? What does it mean for me? What will change in the future?

If there is little certainty about what is to come, you can still bring a form of calm by emphasizing which anchor points will definitely not change.

- **Does a change in one of the PLATO principles suddenly pop up?** Then make that predictable if you can. Explain why the change is necessary and what it means for the rest of the principles.

- **Can't manage to announce changes?** Then provide a small moment to unwind before the child continues with the order of the day.

  HOME: *If a visit from family is cancelled, do a small reception with your own family members with snacks and drinks.*

  SCHOOL: *Need to replace a colleague who is unexpectedly absent? Then start the day with a short, relaxing activity rather than a difficult lesson.*

- **Also make clear what cannot yet be completed and when it can be.** This provides predictability, an overview, and peace of mind.

- **Not sure if your information is correct?** Then better not mention it to avoid the child with autism doubting all your info.

- **When faced with uncertainties or changes, emphasize what is retained in the changed situation.** Some examples: "Your parents will still pick you up at the school gate," "Playtime will still start at 10:30," "Daddy will definitely come and read you a story before bedtime."

STRATEGY 3: Clarify sensory stimuli

In addition to the PLATO principles, it makes sense to provide clarity and predictability about sensory stimuli for many children: their brain cannot always predict these stimuli. That there may be a lot of noise at a children's party or that it may just be unusually quiet in an exam room may seem obvious, but this is not always so for children with autism.

Many educators take a "radical" approach in such cases: they try to eliminate as many sensory stimuli as possible with, for example, headphones or screens in the classroom. While this can certainly be calming for some children in the short term, in a lot of situations this approach is not possible or is unsustainable in the long term. Therefore, it certainly makes sense to also make sensory stimuli predictable as much as possible.

- **Keep the sensory environment uncluttered and sober.** Too many or sudden stimuli are difficult to oversee and difficult to control.

- **Can't adapt the sensory environment?** Then be sure to make it predictable. That way, children with autism know what to expect, and that gives more peace of mind.

  HOME: *Is your child going with you to the store on a Saturday afternoon? Make it predictable that the store may be crowded then and what that means for sensory stimuli.*

  SCHOOL: *Playing tag in gym class? Tell the child that children will run and shout a lot.*

- **Give time to get used to changes in stimuli.** Adjust the pace of activities so children with autism can continue to participate.

- **Offer incentives to those who need them.** Some children with autism need more, not less stimuli to feel good. They may be able to concentrate better in class if they can fiddle with something, nibble on a teething toy, or wiggle on a seat ball.

- **Also adjust the stimuli you create yourself.** Speak at a calm pace at an appropriate volume and announce any touches in advance.

4

AUTONOMY

‘Making decisions yourself gives you back the control you lost due to stress.’

AUTONOMY
WHAT IS IT?

When clarity and predictability are lacking, children with autism experience a lot of confusion and stress. Often, this leads to a feeling of loss of control: it seems as if that stress has completely taken over and is dominating everything. This is a frightening and paralyzing feeling. Some children with autism therefore hardly dare to undertake anything (new): they do not want to go on vacation, even if it is to a nice place, or they refuse assignments in class that they have not done before, even if they have to do with their interests, because "doing something fun" is no substitute for the need for clarity.

The opposite, the feeling of being in control of one's own life, is a very important condition for good development. Self-determination theory calls this *autonomy*. Experiencing some form of control helps children feel good about doing activities, even things they may not like. But many children with autism lack that feeling. And then sometimes they impose that control: they try to bend the situation to their will, because then it will be clear and predictable for them. They are bossy toward other children during a game, but also toward adults by, for example, imposing what food will be at a party. That doesn't mean you should tolerate it. Consider this behavior primarily as a request for predictability and clarity, as you read in the chapter on the first need (being understood).

Give a child with autism autonomy. This includes having a certain amount of freedom, decision-making and choice, but in a defined and predictable framework. If the child is given control over the PLATO principles (persons, locations, activities, time, duration, and organization) it is a double win: it offers predictability and gives the child the feeling of being in control of his life.

Give a child with autism autonomy: a certain amount of freedom, decision-making power and choice, but in a defined and predictable frame.

Gaining control over certain aspects of one's own life is also a necessary step toward more independence. Making or being allowed to make decisions about what they want is not easy for every child. Sometimes the child makes the wrong decision in your eyes and you think, "This will never end well." Children with autism sometimes lack the imagination to properly assess the consequences of their decisions. It is therefore imperative that you weigh the pros and cons of possible decisions together.

Autonomy does not mean "just do anything you want." Children, with and without autism, need direction. But if you provide too much direction, perhaps with the best of intentions, they also lose control of their own lives. Then your well-meaning guidance comes across more as a series of intrusive obligations.

The classmates have a hard time with Jonas. They find him extremely bossy. During breaks, Jonas wants to decide what game to play and who will be on each team. In soccer, he wants to determine who is thief and who is cop etc. It gets to the point where Jonas gets angry when a teammate doesn't pass the ball to someone Jonas points out or when a cop catches a thief too quickly. The kids have to do what he says, but of course they don't just pick that. That is why we see Jonas increasingly hanging out with much younger children. They do still listen to him.

ROB, FOURTH GRADE TEACHER

To provide predictability, my husband and I make a schedule every weekend. Once our daughter Tina has gone to bed on Friday night, we put as many things as possible on a schedule: when we will go to the store, when we will visit Grandma and Grandpa, what we will eat, when Tina can watch TV or play on the iPad. This certainly brought peace to the house for a while, but eventually a bomb exploded. "I don't want to!" she cried when we showed her the schedule.

LIESBET, MOM OF TINA, NINE YEARS OLD

What am I doing this weekend?
1
2
3

HOW CAN YOU SUPPORT THIS NEED?

STRATEGY 1: Connect to the child's experiences

If you want to give a child autonomy, his world and his way of seeing things are central. The child must notice that you take him seriously. Your genuine curiosity not only gives you a sense of trust in the child's abilities, but above all, it gives you a glimpse into his world. It makes it easier for you to understand his point of view. We also call this a Socratic attitude: just as Socrates acted almost naively and ignorantly to extract knowledge from his interlocutor, you ask the child concrete questions about his experience.

- **Create a set ritual for asking about experiences:** deliberately make time to probe with clear questions about how the child experienced his day, weekend or playtime, for example. Schedule that at a set time.

  HOME: *End the dinner with a conversation moment under the heading "My Day." Each family member draws a paper from a "conversation jar" containing questions such as, "This is what I liked doing most today," "I heard something funny today, namely ...," "I was also kind of angry today because ..."*

  SCHOOL: *At the end of the day, have a child award stars to the different lessons and breaks of the school day: three stars for the funniest moments, one for the difficult ones.*

- **Ask genuinely curious questions.** Don't be satisfied with a short answer. For example, if a child only liked the playtime, first ask what was fun about the playtime: "Who did you play with? What game did you play? How did the game go?"

- **But also allow openness to what was difficult.** In doing so, avoid the direct "why" question, but translate it in a concrete way.

  HOME: *Do not ask, "Why did you get so angry at school today?" but rather, "What exercises were difficult?" or, "What did you find not so clear today?"*

  SCHOOL: *Do not ask, "Why didn't you do your homework?" but rather, "What questions did you find difficult?" or, "What did you do at home last night?"*

- **Keep your opinion or judgment to yourself.** This conversation is not about what the child did right or wrong, good or bad, but rather how the child experienced something. By unintentionally correcting a child anyway, you make some feelings, behaviors, or preferences taboo.

STRATEGY 2: Offer choices

Choices provide the necessary sense of control: "I still have something to decide for myself." With choices, you give a child a say. You decide yourself what a child can decide. The PLATO principles are an ideal start.

- **If you want to provide predictability in a daily or weekly schedule, give a child a say in who, where, what, when, and how.**

- **Make the choices clear by presenting them concretely and making them visual if possible.**

  HOME: *"This weekend we are going to visit Grandma. You can choose when: Saturday afternoon, Sunday morning, or Sunday evening," "Today we are going to clean up your room. You can choose who helps you: Mom or Dad, or maybe you prefer to do it alone," "After dinner you will do your homework. Would you rather do it in your room, in the living room, or in the kitchen?"*

  SCHOOL: *"You have to do these three exercises. You may choose which exercise to start with," "Today we are doing a task in pairs. Who do you want to work with: Els, Kris, or Tim?" "We will now fill in these sums. Do you prefer to do it with a pen or a pencil?"*

- **Don't overdo it with the number of options.** Try to provide three options at a time. More options do not necessarily give more freedom, and children with autism sometimes lose the overview.

- **Discuss any pros and cons of the options before asking the child to choose one.**

  HOME: *"If we go visit Grandma on Sunday night, there might not be time left to watch TV afterward," "If you prefer to do your homework in the kitchen, you can. But Mom and Dad will be cleaning up there, too, so there might be more noise."*

  SCHOOL: *"If you want to complete the exercises with a pen, it's harder to correct any mistakes," "If you do the exercises you're good at first, you'll have plenty of time afterward to tackle the difficult ones."*

- **Ask for regular feedback on the choices the child made and why they made or did not make a particular choice.** Sometimes there is a reason behind this that gives you a glimpse into the child's experience.

- **Also make it clear when a child has no choice and why that is so. In that case, try to suggest a "secondary choice."** For example, the child does not have a choice about whether or not to do his homework, but perhaps where, when, or with whom. The child does not have a choice about when you will visit Grandma, but possibly what game he will play there.

STRATEGY 3: Let children be themselves

Because children with autism perceive and understand the world differently, they sometimes exhibit behaviors that you might label as strange. In the first chapter on the need to be understood, you already read that a focus on the cause of that behavior and a look at all the positive moments is more beneficial. But in addition, ask the question, "For whom is the behavior actually a problem?" If the child is saying or doing something that is not harmful to the child or those around him, should something change?

- **Don't correct the child's behavior all the time.** Some children with autism may hum often, while others flap their hands or rock their chairs. This can be a very effective way to discharge stress at times and an expression of joy or positive excitement at other times.
- **Do you think such behavior will lead to strange looks from other children?** Then offer the child a safe place where they can and may be themselves for a while, out of sight of others.
- **Does the child talk about his interest all the time?** Avoid a, "Shut up about that!" but agree on a moment where you genuinely make time to listen. Schedule that visually in a planner.
- **Does the child have set routines that sometimes take some time?** Recognize that this provides peace of mind and give the child time to carry them out rather than blocking them out or rushing them.

HOME: *Does your child first want to put all the stuffed animals in a row before the light is switched off at bedtime? Schedule this into a clear evening ritual.*

SCHOOL: *Does the child want to organize all the ballpoint pens on their school desk before starting a task? Then let them go to class a few minutes early.*

5

CONNECTION

“I am here for you, and you are here for me. Each in our own way, as best we can.”

CONNECTION
WHAT IS IT?

Dealing with others is often difficult for autistic children. After all, other people (classmates, family members, parents, teachers, friends) are the most unpredictable and unclear pieces of their environment. No two people are alike. Everyone does things in his or her own way. What one person likes, another just finds stupid. What makes one person sad sometimes makes another laugh. Social interaction requires lightning-fast flexibility to respond to what our brain predicts to see in the other person. But it is not because that is difficult for children with autism that they do not want social contact. They, too, want to belong and need connection.

Connection is fundamentally about feeling a secure, close bond. But the social activities which create connection tend to be less structured, less predictable, and also brimming with unwritten, vague, and abstract rules.

Connection has a strong mutual component: I am here for you and you are here for me. Each in our own way, as best we can. So it's not about "everyone else has to adapt to you," nor is it about "you have to behave the way everyone else wants you to." Much more important is respecting each other's needs and being mindful of each other's strengths. If you can share those needs and use those strengths together with and for another, then you are working on connection.

That mutual component also means that a one-sided view of connection can have the opposite effect. Just sitting together and chatting, a nice party with lots of friends and family, a play time when children can hang out together nicely—what you consider cozy, fun, or nice—can take on a completely different meaning for an autistic child. Or it can only become cozy, fun, and nice when the basic conditions for autism friendliness are met.

Finding security in social contacts: predictability and clarity are essential.

Connection is not an absolute quantitative concept. Having many friends is not always better than having a few good ones, and frequently doing things together is not always better than occasionally. Quality is more important. For an autistic child, that often comes down to the security he or she can find in social interactions, and in that, again, predictability and clarity are central.

Family parties always cause stress. Leah doesn't see her nephews and nieces very often, and she wants to play with them so much, but things often go wrong after only ten minutes. Add to that the fact that there are a lot of people in our living room during a party, all kinds of conversations get mixed up, and all our family routines no longer count. So it becomes too much for Leah. "When are you all leaving?" she shouted through the living room at her birthday party.

ELAINE, MOM OF LEAH, TEN YEARS OLD

A Monday-morning circle discussion was always awkward for Louie. The children would sit together for a few moments to socialize before the school day really started, and I would ask who wanted to tell me something about their weekend. Louie never stayed in the circle. While a classmate was telling something, he got up and sat down at his school desk already. Since we established a clear turn order and made clear agreements about how long each child is allowed to talk, Louie does manage to stay in the circle.

PETER, SECOND GRADE TEACHER

HOW CAN YOU SUPPORT THIS NEED?

STRATEGY 1: Make social activities safe

When your head is full of questions and consequently stress bubbles up, it is difficult to experience connection during social activities. Some children respond by dominating social interaction; others drop out and stay on the sidelines. Through predictability and clarity, you can make social contacts safer.

- **Make clear in advance who will be present at an activity.** Distinguish between "participants" and "attendees" if necessary.

  HOME: *A family party at a restaurant? Make it clear to your child who is coming, but also that there will be other people in the restaurant who are not part of your family.*

  SCHOOL: *A school trip to an amusement park? Clearly agree with the child what you want to do with the class group and what they may do individually. Also make the obvious clear: there will be other schools at the amusement park.*

- **Clarify certain (behavioral) expectations.** Good agreements and rules can help. That way the child knows what is expected of him, but also what he can expect from others.

- **Offer predictability in the program:** who will do what and when?

- **Is predictability difficult because you yourself don't know what is to happen or who will be there?** Then focus on people who will definitely attend and make the child feel secure. Not sure about that either? Explore the possibility of having a buddy or confidant join the social activity.

- **Plan activities where social interaction varies.** Not everything has to be with everyone. Find out what the child can handle in which situation.

  HOME: *Provide a game you can do together with your child to fill the waiting time at the restaurant table, as well as something your child can do alone. Remember that drawing a picture while sis is also drawing one is not all alone. Sharing materials, such as crayons, is also social interaction.*

  SCHOOL: *A conversation about the weekend in pairs is sometimes easier than in a large group. Make clear arrangements: Who starts? How long are you allowed to talk? When are you allowed to ask questions to each other?*

STRATEGY 2: Enjoy in moderation

Despite the many ways you can make a social activity safer, you can't completely eliminate confusion, ambiguity, and stress. Every party is different; every group task is still just a little different from the last. That doesn't mean it's better to avoid all social activities, but you can think about "dosed enjoyment."

- **Allow your child to avoid the biggest (social) crowds at the start of the activities.** This can be done either by arriving just a little earlier so your child can see everyone else arrive one at a time, or a little later so everyone is already somewhat settled.

- **Again, give choices to the child:** clarify what parts of the activity there are, and give your child a say in which parts he or she does and prefers not to do in group.

  HOME: *Clarify the program of a birthday party: arrival of people, eating cake, opening presents, playing a game ... In which parts does your child like to participate and in which can he stay alone in his room for a while?*

  SCHOOL: *Let the child choose whether to spend recess in the large group on the playground or play a game with one other child in a room inside.*

- Agree on a clear "escape scenario." What if things go wrong? Where can your child go then? What can they do there? How long can they stay there?

- **Plan time for relaxation, both before and after social activity.**

7
16
5

STRATEGY 2: Offer alternatives.

Creating connection goes beyond making adjustments to social activities. Sharing strengths or interests with each other also creates a bond. But even each other's presence, without all kinds of interaction involved, can create a positive feeling for both.

- **An "escape scenario" does not always mean that the child must disappear from the social situation altogether.**

- **A concrete alternative can help and still make the child part of the social activity.**

  HOME: *Let your child make or read something during a family gathering. In doing so, also agree that he or she may show it to everyone or tell something about it when it is finished.*

  SCHOOL: *A similar alternative can be done during a group discussion about the weekend or during class. Fellow students can then ask questions about the child's drawing (and thus ask how the weekend went or what they liked best in the past lesson).*

- **Tackle social activities according to an "apart together" system:** some parts of the activity the child does together, others separately. Start together and finish together. Agree on a clear time frame.

  HOME: *First divide blocks between brother and sister. Then each builds their own structure in their own place. Then they show everything to each other and tell what they made.*

SCHOOL: *In group assignments, divide tasks among group members based on individual competencies and create a clear schedule together.*

- **Organize activities around common interests where the child can tell or do something with "like-minded people."** Dare to organize this regardless of age.

  HOME: *Does your child have a specific interest in a particular subject? Also check with organizations for adults if the child may join (occasionally).*

  SCHOOL: *Organize clubs across class groups that may meet during play times around a theme. Establish clear agreements and rules.*

6

GOOD AGREEMENTS AND RULES

“Autism-friendly agreements and rules make social interaction a lot more fun.”

GOOD AGREEMENTS AND RULES
WHAT IS IT?

Our society is full of rules and agreements that ensure that we can live together in a predictable way. Some of these are strict, visualized, and clearly agreed upon; others are looser, less visible, and dependent on the situation. They clarify what behavior is or is not expected in a given context. In this way, they contribute to clarity, predictability, and certainty. This applies to everyone, whether you are autistic or not.

Children with autism do not always spontaneously and intuitively sense what behavior is or is not expected of them. Because their brain takes less account of the context, they sometimes exhibit behavior that is quite normal in one situation but rather unexpected or inappropriate in another. In the second case, they receive reactions from others, which in turn are unexpected and difficult for them to understand. This can create a vicious cycle of confusion, frustration, and challenging behavior.

Autism-friendly agreements and rules help an autistic child. They make predictable what behavior the child can expect from others and what behavior is expected from them. This makes social intercourse, at home or at school, a lot more fun. Nevertheless, rules and agreements are sometimes used only as a reaction to behavior. Unfortunately, this is pointless. For example, if a child is full of stress because they have not understood something, because something is unpredictable, or because their brain reacts heavily to a sensory stimulus and then says something inappropriate, a rule like, "Don't swear," rarely helps. After all, everything starts with being understood: addressing the cause of the stress then automatically produces behavioral change.

Give the child a say in the agreements. Then the motivation is greater to follow them.

Sometimes a child is supposed to follow rules, at home or at school. These are imposed from a higher level (for example, by you as a teacher or parent). A possible disadvantage of rules is that the child is less motivated to follow them because they have little say in the matter. You might then try to soften that by offering rewards if the child will follow the rules anyway. Some teachers or parents are more likely to want to enforce their rules by punishment.

Agreements do give a child a say. They are drawn up in consultation. So the child does not determine the agreements, but they certainly have a voice in them. As a result, the child has a greater motivation to follow those agreements. There is also more social control with agreements: classmates or family members are more likely to point out to each other behavior that goes against the agreements.

A combination of rules and agreements is often the way to go. From the previous needs, you can see that clarity and predictability are crucial. But clear rules and agreements are only the beginning. Like many other children, autistic children sometimes do things that go against these clear rules or agreements. Sometimes this happens with a lot of resistance. As always, it is then important to follow a strategy that focuses not so much on the behavior that a child in resistance exhibits, but on the various causes of the resistance. The more realistic the self-esteem, the happier the child feels.

Indoors we take off our shoes, that's a rule in our family. On the kitchen door hangs a pictogram that reminds everyone, but especially Lauren, of that rule. But when we have visitors, we push the rule aside. Then I have my heels on and Dad wears his sneakers. "Why have shoes in the house today and not again tomorrow?" Lauren asks angrily.

KAREN, MOM OF LAUREN, EIGHT YEARS OLD

Jonathan had a tantrum at school. For the third time, he didn't get to class until after the bell rang. The rule at school is that he then has to go to detention, but Jonathan thinks this is ridiculous. "I couldn't help it if I still had to go to the bathroom, could I? And another time a friend had to ask something important." Each time he had a reason why he was late, but it didn't count.

FREDERICK, TEACHER IN MIDDLE SCHOOL

Monday
8:00
garage
Monday
10:00
dentist
Monday

HOW CAN YOU SUPPORT THIS NEED?

STRATEGY 1: Tackle amotivation

Resistance can manifest itself in many different ways. You might hear a deep sigh when you want to set up rules and agreements. "I can't do all that," "That is much too difficult for me," "I don't understand any of it." This communication is also revealing behavior. In these cases we speak of amotivation: a child with autism does not want to or cannot follow these rules and agreements because there are reasons why he does not succeed (anymore).

- **So first of all, make sure you have autism-friendly rules and agreements according to the strategies you could read in the section on the need for "clarity."** Rules that are difficult to understand can never be followed.
- **Also make it clear how a rule or agreement should be followed:** what do you expect an autistic child to do when they need to be quiet, ask permission, eat nicely, play together well?
- **Ask yourself whether this is actually (already) feasible for the child.** Some rules presuppose many social-interaction, communication, or stress-management skills that an autistic child does not always (already) have mastered.
- **So reward (or punish) thoughtfully:** rewarding (or punishing) a child for something they cannot (yet) do is downright unfair and will cause a lot of frustration.

- **Limit rules and agreements in number.** After all, you can't put every expected behavior into rules. Children (with autism) can more easily follow five rules or agreements than twenty.

- **Also refer to the rules and agreements when the child follows them well.** That way the child doesn't see them as something negative or limiting. This increases the sense of competence in those who are willing to follow the rules while sometimes not yet succeeding.

STRATEGY 2: Handle rebellious resistance thoughtfully

A completely different reason for resistance to rules and agreements has less to do with wording or feasibility and more to do with the position of authority. "Following rules is for suckers," "It's cool to disobey," "You don't even follow the rules yourselves!" "You have nothing to say to me." We call this rebellious resistance. It is a form of disobedience to authority (parent, teacher, educator): "Just because you are making me do it, I won't do it!"

- **Especially with rebellious resistance, maintain a healthy balance between rules on the one hand and agreements on the other** so that the child feels they are being heard.

- **Again, rules and agreements must be achievable,** not only for the autistic child, but also for you and your colleagues or partner. Rules or agreements that for whatever reason are not followed by every teacher or both parents create more ambiguity. Be a cohesive team!

- **"Choose your battles" is therefore an important principle in rebellious resistance.** It is also easier for you and your colleagues or partner to follow fewer rules and agreements.

- **Some children use resistance to the rules as a way to gain more social status.** "It's cool to disobey," "Doing homework is for suckers," "Look what I dare do." In this way, they try to make all kinds of compensation for difficult social skills. So help autistic children apply alternatives: "What does being cool mean to you?" "In what ways can you be cool without being disobedient?"

- **Keep looking beyond behavior.** Some autistic children camouflage amotivation ("I can't do this") with rebellious resistance ("Rules are stupid"). Be careful and patient to explore together what is already working well (which rules are being followed well) and what is going less smoothly. By starting from what works, you create openings through which the children dare to leave their camouflage behind.

STRATEGY 3: Think about reflective resistance

Autistic children may also exhibit a third form of resistance to rules and agreements: they call them "nonsense" or "ridiculous" even if they are formulated in an autism-friendly way. Rules and agreements are about predictable social interaction that benefits both the autistic child and others. But in some situations, that benefit is not so obvious to a child with autism. It might even be that the child sees only limitations for themselves and benefits for others in those rules. It is then not surprising that the child will not follow such rules or agreements. This is what is called *reflective resistance*.

Especially in stressful situations, and this is precisely where many rules and agreements pop up, it is not natural for autistic children to take into account the needs of (sometimes not even present) others. So it is important to invest enough time in a safe, calm situation to make sense of the functionality of rules and agreements. In other words, before you start listing rules and agreements, it's better to first explain why they make sense in general and the usefulness of a specific rule or agreement in particular. For children without autism, this is easily logical or understandable, but this is not always obvious to autistic people.

- **Take the time to explain the usefulness of rules and agreements,** in a clear way, with unambiguous, positive, and visible communication.
- **Don't engage in a personal battle with something like, "You have to do that because I say so!"** Keep everything objective and neutral.

- **Emphasize especially the advantages of following rules rather than the disadvantages of not following them.** That, too, is positive, autism-friendly communication.

  HOME: *"Take off your shoes, otherwise the house will get dirty," is not as motivational as, "Take off your shoes so your playroom stays neat."*

  SCHOOL: *"If you are not quiet in class, you will get a punishment," is better stated as, "If you are quiet, we can all work quietly."*

- **When clarifying the benefits of following rules, focus especially on the benefits to the autistic child.** Give a reason why the child is better off following a rule, and how the rule contributes to benefit the child himself. Following rules just because others want you to does not motivate.

- **The sooner the child can experience that benefit, the better.** So avoid reasoning such as, "Later on in life, you must follow that rule too."

- **If following a rule or agreement in different situations is beneficial to an autistic child, be sure to emphasize it.**

• work in silence
= work better
• keep the sofa tidy
= find things faster

7

POSITIVE SELF-ESTEEM

"Self-confidence grows out of a recognition of successes and difficulties."

POSITIVE SELF-ESTEEM
WHAT IS IT?

Because autistic children have a hard time spontaneously and intuitively understanding what is going on around them, problems with communication, social contacts, and acting flexibly crop up. Just about all the main characteristics of autism revolve around such difficulties: not being able to do something well, being weaker than others in certain things, being rigid and inflexible.

This entire book tries to emphasize that autistic children are first and foremost wonderful children who also possess many good qualities, and with the aid of clarity and predictability can handle quite a lot. However it is not always easy for them to recognize these qualities and their potential. Many autistic children do notice at a certain age that they are different, but mainly in what they can do less fluently than their peers. They see how other children make friends seemingly effortlessly, play together, understand what the teacher says, and are not bothered by all kinds of sensory stimuli. On the other hand, autistic children are less able to see how they themselves evolve, what they are growing into, what they are capable of, and where their strengths lie. After all, that requires a solid chunk of cognitive processes within their imagination, such as self-assessment and metacognition.

Children compare themselves to each other in a rather superficial way to determine whether they are good or bad at something. Such comparisons usually do not turn out well for autistic children. Because they mainly see what others are good at and have less eye for their own development, they often consider themselves inferior to children without autism.

An inferior self-image is a brake on personal growth. Try to let the child experience successes, and then explore together what contributed to those successes.

An inferior self-esteem is a brake on personal growth. Try to let the child experience successes, and then explore together what contributed to those successes.

Many of the needs described earlier already indirectly avoid a negative self-esteem. And this is important, because an inferior self-esteem is a strong brake on personal growth. It leads to a lack of self-confidence, it creates fear of failure, and it takes away all the positive emotions that arise when successes are achieved. A long-term negative self-esteem leads to depression in many cases. Unfortunately, this can happen even at a young age.

If you want to do something about that, it does not mean that you have to deny or minimize all the difficulties that autism presents. First, try to let the child experience successes to build self-confidence, and then explore together what contributed to those successes.

By the way, the same also applies to autistic children who (perhaps not always rightly) radiate the opposite and thus feel successful in everything. Some of them overestimate themselves enormously. The same cognitive processes lie at the base: if you do not recognize any of your weaker sides, this will eventually lead to difficulties. But be alert: this self-overestimation can also be a form of camouflage: I say that I can and know it all, because otherwise I might notice that I am not very good at certain thing.

So working on a positive self-esteem means building success on the basis of one's own strengths, with the help of clarity and predictability to compensate for weaknesses.

Stan gives up quickly if something goes wrong. He tries once, but if it doesn't work, he gets angry. Especially on himself. "I can't do anything!" We notice that he doesn't even get around to trying anymore.

RICHARD, DAD OF STAN, ELEVEN YEARS OLD

Christofer is bored in class. If I explain something to him and he understands it, he considers the subject matter or the exercise already known. He doesn't see that something must be practiced or studied to remember it as well.

TANIA, FIFTH GRADE TEACHER

litter box changed
helped Mom a lot
went to a family party
1
room tidied up
nice drawing
make sister laugh
say what's bothering me

HOW CAN YOU SUPPORT THIS NEED?

STRATEGY 1: Aim for success

Achieving (small) successes contributes to a positive self-esteem. But it is not always easy to find the right balance between a task or activity that is too easy and one that is still just within one's current capabilities.

- **First make sure that the PLATO principles are clearly filled in for the task or activity to be performed.** Without autism friendly tools, such as clarity and predictability, chances for a successful experience will be small. For example, do you want a child to experience success during a math exercise? Then first make sure that it is clear what the child has to do, how the exercise is structured, where and when it is to be done, and possibly with whom.

- **For children with low self-esteem, provide multiple short tasks or activities rather than a few larger ones.** After all, every little task, every exercise, every activity can be a success.

- **Divide larger exercises or activities into partial steps** so the child and you can get a better idea of what he or she can already do and what is still difficult.

  HOME: *The task, "Slice the mushrooms," can be rephrased as, "Get the knife and cutting board ready," "Find the mushrooms in the refrigerator and put them on the counter," "Slice the mushrooms."*

SCHOOL: *Go from, "Give a presentation," as an assignment to, "Find images online," "Print images," "Glue images on a summary sheet," "Note what you see in each image."*

- **Use a step-by-step plan, not just to clarify how a task or exercise should be done.** Also have the child check off or cross out each step that is done, with the message, "This step is done!"

- **Make it clear in advance with autism-friendly criteria when a task or activity has been done well (enough)** so that the child can evaluate himself afterward. If you often hear, "Is that good?" then the criteria were probably not clear.

  HOME: *Make, "Slice mushrooms," more concrete so that the task is easier to evaluate afterward: "Slice each mushroom into four equal pieces."*

  SCHOOL: *Make, "Do an online image search," more concrete by specifying, for example, "Find three pictures and two drawings."*

- **Make mistakes.** It may sound silly, but by making a mistake yourself once in a while and solving it, you show that mistakes can be fixed. This is especially important for children with fear of failure. With such children, it is better to focus on dealing with mistakes than on achieving a good result.

STRATEGY 2: Compare in a fair way

Comparing with others is a way of estimating your performance. But what exactly are you comparing: the result, the effort? Comparing is not automatically a bad thing.

- **First, compare intrapersonally: the child's own learning process and growth.** Emphasize after a new success that the child did something he or she could not do yesterday.
- **Go into detail about success:** "What helped you do this so well?" "How did you go about it?" "Did you practice a lot?"
- **Emphasize previous attempts: sometimes the child does not succeed at something the first time.** Compliment the child on his perseverance (more on that in a later chapter) and again ask what helped him to persevere.
- **Focus on the child's own part in his success.** Some autistic children shift the cause of success to others: "It only worked because you helped!" Counter this with all the child's actions: "You asked for help," "You did a good job executing my tips!"
- **Does the child appear to be comparing interpersonally (himself with others) anyway?** Then focus not on the outcome, but on the process that others (perhaps) went through: "How would your friend have learned that?" "What would have helped your brother do this so well?"

- **Don't always demonstrate perfection yourself.** This sometimes makes the difference very big and is more likely to cause despondency: "I'm never going to be able to do this as well, quickly, beautifully, etc. as you." Emphasize your learning process, what helped you, how often you practiced, etc.

  HOME: *Does your child help in the kitchen? Occasionally slice the onion a little slower and tell how you learned to do it yourself.*

  Is your child helping wash the car? Then talk about why you put how much soap in the water and why it's best to start at the top. Also, let your child discover that a chamois cloth absorbs more water than a duster.

  SCHOOL: *Complete an exercise on the board by yourself. Then verbalize your thinking process. Show that you also search before you find something.*

Oops, is this correct?
:5
x12
?
distance
20km
4 km
42 km
time
25 min
5 min
hour
:5
x12

STRATEGY 3: Compare in a fair way

Not every learning process goes smoothly, and sometimes it takes a long time to make progress. If there is not an immediate result noticeable, autistic children sometimes fail to see their own small steps.

- **Visualize every small piece of progress. Children often know this from (computer) games:** characters "leveling up," collecting more "power points," cars getting better tires over the course of a game. These are all concrete visualizations of growth that can also be used in activities to signify progress. This could be things like stronger armor for a knight when the child has put on his clothes alone, a gold star on a good test at school, extra "energy" points after a good soccer game. Perhaps the child's interests or favorite games also contain such metaphors?

- **Collect successes in a glass jar: with the child, write each success on a colored note and put it in the jar.** Over time, the jar visibly fills up.

- **Use different-colored notes for different domains.** This way you broaden the child's horizons: you show that not everything goes badly if things are a bit off in one domain.

  HOME: *Use notes with a different color for schoolwork, household chores, sports/hobbies, family and friends.*

  SCHOOL: *Use different colors for different school subjects or different forms of work: individual work, class work, leisure, group work in pairs, etc.*

- **Celebrate successes.** Plan fun time together to celebrate personal growth. Do something fun together rather than give material rewards.

8

CONTENTMENT

“When autistic children feel good, they can more easily survive a confusing world.”

CONTENTMENT
WHAT IS IT?

Children who feel good can handle much more than children who do not feel good. In this they are no different from adults. Because of their different way of thinking, the world is very unpredictable and confusing for autistic children. But if they feel good, they can survive that world more easily. It is also perfectly possible that then they won't be bothered at all by loud racing games or music, whereas otherwise they find it so difficult to tolerate noise (vacuum cleaner, lawnmower).

Children who feel good about themselves are also open to new things. Feeling good promotes learning. If they do not feel good, there is little room to learn because there is little energy. Learning always means getting out of the comfort zone, but that only works if there is a comfort zone. Autistic children who have no or too little comfort easily show resistance to learning and to all other new things that require energy from them.

Trying to make autistic children feel good does not mean that you should stop challenging them or avoid any unpleasantness at all costs with them. Autism should not become an excuse to avoid challenges and difficult situations. Growing always hurts a little. So does growing up. The key is to find a good balance between indulging and challenging. The happiest people are not those who have no problems (do such people even exist?), but those who can handle and solve their problems. By the way, in order to cope well with unpleasant feelings, children must also sometimes experience those feelings. If you are never angry or disappointed, you cannot learn to deal with those feelings.

A predictable and clear world is the greatest source of contentment for these children.

Trying to make autistic children feel good means making sure they have enough energy to ride out the sometimes difficult rides you ask of them. But also that they can refuel at regular intervals during those difficult rides. A predictable and clear world is the greatest source of well-being for them, no matter how much spoiling contributes to feeling good (through a nice ice cream, not having to do homework for once, being allowed to stay up longer, a day at an amusement park). You can never spoil them enough with clarity and security.

Being understood, predictability, and clarity are the foundation of feeling good in autistic children. Without that foundation, the following strategies are often nothing more than a drop in the bucket.

Jessica was allowed to skip one task every week at school. She didn't have to do that one. We did that to give her a little more rest. But soon she let us know that she didn't want too many exceptions and that skipping a task didn't actually give her much peace of mind. What would work was a little more clarity on what was most important in the subject matter and therefore where she would best put her time while studying and where it was better not to.

JONAS, MIDDLE SCHOOL TEACHER

Karim is easily bothered by noises. The lawnmower, the vacuum cleaner—he even finds the bubbling of the coffee maker unpleasant and disturbing, especially if I make coffee while he is busy doing something that requires a lot of energy from him, such as his homework. Then he puts on his headphones. But when Karim watches YouTube videos of Formula 1 races, the television can't be loud enough. Racing cars, that's his main interest. We once took him to a racetrack for his birthday. Despite all the crowds, noise, and racket there, Karim didn't complain once about noise.

SAÏD, DAD OF KARIM, ELEVEN YEARS OLD

HOW CAN YOU SUPPORT THIS NEED?

STRATEGY 1: Discover (together) the well-being profile

What makes autistic children feel good is not always the same as what works for children without autism. For example, an autistic child may enjoy watching children play together on the playground more than participating. And there are also autistic children who relax nicely by solving difficult math riddles and problems.

- **Complete the feel-good questionnaire, together with the child if necessary.** This questionnaire helps you discover what can contribute to making the child feel good. You can find it as a free download in the online shop of one of the authors of this book: https://autismincontext.be/browse/downloads.

- **Be aware that sensory stimuli can also make one feel good.** There are lots of questionnaires to identify the problems of autistic children with sensory stimuli, but it may be more rewarding to look (preferably with the child) for the stimuli that make the child feel good. What kind of light? What taste or flavors? What clothing fabric?

- Two know more than one, and three know more than two. **Also ask others who know the child (well) what they think makes the child feel good.** Perhaps your child's teacher could also fill out the feel-good questionnaire.

- Some children with autism can draw what makes them feel good better than talking about it. **Have them draw a picture of the ideal world:** What does it look like to them? What is there or just barely there? Who gives them contentment? What does the child do in that ideal world?

- Sometimes an autistic child may have difficulty indicating for himself what makes him feel good. **Then do feel-good exercises together to discover which things make them feel good.**

  HOME: *Offer your child five songs or sounds (waves, forest sounds, etc.) and ask which of them calms him down.*

  SCHOOL: *Provide ballpoint pens that differ in thickness, texture, and color. Have the child write something with each of these ballpoint pens. Then ask which ballpoint pen feels best and which one the child prefers to write with.*

STRATEGY 2: Deploy (specific) interests

Autistic children can have unusual or very specific interests and experience them intensively. Such specific interests have a function: in an ocean of uncertainty, these children create an island of security by intensely immersing themselves in one piece of that unpredictable world. Doing something they love not only makes them feel good, but it also motivates them and causes them to push their limits.

- **Map out the interests of the child.** Also communicate them to anyone who interacts or works with the child, and ask them to match those interests.

- If an autistic child has a very unusual, special or specific interest, do not try to diminish or take it away. **Work in small steps toward broadening or making the limited or unusual interest more habitual.**

- **Let the child's special interest "infect" the learning objectives.**

  HOME: *A child with a special interest in fish will find learning to clean up toys a lot more fun if all the drawers and boxes for the toys have names of fish.*

  SCHOOL: *An autistic child with will feel more comfortable learning to write if they are allowed to write words related to their interests.*

- **Plan on being engaged with the interests and clarify that planning.** This way the child has the reassurance that he will indeed be allowed to be engaged in that interest, and also sees when he can and when he cannot.

STRATEGY 3: Plan the relaxation

A child knows if they are feeling well when they can read their own body. That is something that many autistic children are not able to do well. This can cause not only problems in potty training or eating, but also in emotion regulation. This manifests itself, for example, in a sudden change in mood: like a bolt from the blue, the cheerful child suddenly becomes an angry child.

Some children can assess their own feelings a little better, but they do not have the skills to organize or ask for relaxing and feel-good activities themselves. They walk on the tips of their toes for too long, until their moods crash too.

- **Proactively organize feel-good activities in the daily planning.** Have the child do those activities even if they indicate they are doing well at that time.
- **Begin and end learning activities with a short, relaxing, feel-good routine.** This can be a breathing or other relaxation exercise, but equally a nice song, verse, or favorite puzzle.
- **Make a feel-good box with the child.** The box contains objects that make the child feel good: a fidget, a picture the child likes to look at, a favorite sound, an object with the child's favorite smell. Teach the child to take something from the box as soon as he or she feels some tension or overstimulation. Give the box a permanent place in the house. It can perhaps be taken to school as well. Plan to introduce the use of the box yourself at regular intervals, such as before or after a meal, if the child does not initiate it himself.

- **Always end the (school) day with a feel-good day end.** This can be done, for example, with a pride journal in which the child notes something each night that made him proud that day. It can also be done with the "like of the day" or "joke of the day" or a relaxation exercise.

9

MEANING

"Doing meaningful things contributes to growth."

MEANING

WHAT IS IT?

If you want to save autistic children stress, you may quickly think of doing fun things. Fun activities, games, or strategies in the classroom certainly come to mind. You have read in the previous chapters that this can create more connection. You can also use it to visualize the competences of children with autism and to make them feel good or better.

But that doesn't mean you can just aim for fun to stimulate, motivate, or help children grow. Even more, if you want to make everything "fun," it is best to keep in mind there are also pitfalls. For example, you might unintentionally create the expectation, "Everything is fun. What's not fun, you don't have to do." As nice as that sounds, it does not correspond to the reality of (later) life.

Don't just aim for fun to stimulate or motivate autistic children. Help them see the relevance of activities or tasks.

After all, a child is also expected to perform activities or tasks that he or she finds boring or stupid. A second pitfall of focusing too much on pleasure is in the pleasure itself: the more the environment links everything to what the child finds fun or interesting, the greater the chance that one day they will simply get tired of it. Especially if the environment also starts linking those "stupid" tasks or activities to the child's interests, the child might develop an aversion to those interests. A final difficulty with fun is that it is very individual. What one child likes, another may find boring (or vice versa). If you live or work with groups of (autistic) children, this variation in interests is not always easy.

But the self-determination theory on which this book is based offers a solution: if you want to get autistic children motivated and increase their well-being, you don't have to aim only at fun but can also get to work with "meaningful" activities.

There are many positive emotions and satisfaction in those tasks or assignments. They involve doing meaningful things (useful for the child themselves or for another), or things that they may not find super fun but in which they see the relevance of.

Understanding the relevance of certain activities or tasks is not always easy for autistic children. This can have different causes. Often they come down to a lack of imagination. Sometimes the relevance lies further in the future (studying to get a diploma later), sometimes the relevance lies in a positive feeling with someone else (saying "thank you" to make someone else happy), and sometimes the relevance is rarely noticeable or only in one specific situation (learning French because one day you might go on vacation to Paris).

A lot of kids express this lack of meaningfulness with the famous "why?" question. "Why do I have to clean my room?" "Why do I have to do homework?" "Why do I have to brush my teeth?" "Why do I need to listen to others?" The list is endless. In autistic children, these questions quickly pop up when the answer refers to something in the future or someone else. Such why questions do not automatically imply that these children do not want to do anything whose meaning lies in the future or with someone else. Quite the contrary, in fact. But that meaning must be clear and predictable. An answer like, "You have to clean up your room because I say so," or, "You have to do homework because you must," may bring clarity (though it is questionable) but not meaning. It does not clarify relevance to an autistic child.

Jana played volleyball in a club. She loved it, but after a serious injury she had to rehabilitate for months. At first she was still eager to go watch her teammates' trainings and matches, but that made her increasingly sad: she could not play yet. But her coach gave her a new meaning during the period of her rehabilitation: during practices, she became his assistant. She set up cones on the court for certain exercises, she collected the balls, she kept track of the scores. That's how Jana felt useful and valuable to the team.

TIM, DAD OF JANA, FOURTEEN YEARS OLD

Ken thinks neat writing is pointless: "I can read it myself, so it's good." He just didn't think it was important enough to write neatly so the teacher could read it too. But when we could show him the benefit for himself, his motivation grew. We told him if he would write his birthday gift wish list neatly, family and friends could see properly what presents to buy for him. If he wrote jokes neatly, others could laugh at them. If he wrote the shopping list neatly, his parents would not forget his favorite cookies in the store. And notes with secret messages, his friends can't read until they are neatly written!

JO, THIRD GRADE TEACHER

HOW CAN YOU SUPPORT THIS NEED?

STRATEGY 1: Do functional things

Autistic children need to fill their (free) time. Doing nothing for a while or waiting is often very stressful. Doing something "fun" can help, but functional activities are at least as useful.

- **At free times, allow the child to help with (household) chores appropriate to his competencies.** Give him the necessary direction and support according to the Plato principles.

- **In such activities, emphasize the functionality for the child:** tell them what it gains.

  HOME: *Helping to cook? 'Then you can choose the kind of pasta you like best.' Help put away the laundry? 'Then you can put your favorite shirts on top so you can find them quickly.'*

  SCHOOL: *Make the link between lesson content and the daily life of the autistic child. It may be clear to you what the child can do with math or geography, but it is not always so clear to the child himself.*

- **In such a functional explanation, emphasize what the child can gain in the present** and not too much on what's to gain "later on in life, when you grow up."

- **Consider a why question not as a lack of motivation but as a lack of clarity.**

STRATEGY 2: Reward thoughtfully

If the meaning or purpose of a task or activity is not clear to an autistic child, you may sometimes rely on rewards, just a little too quickly. Rewards are functional: they are fun for the child himself and they have an effect in the present (or very quickly anyway). They are an easy answer to the question, "Why do I have to do this?" But rewards overturn the whole meaning of the activity or task. They are behavioral responses that sometimes ignore the needs of the autistic child. Rewards are not useless, but they require some reflection in advance.

- **Don't start rewards right away if the child finds something unclear or they don't quite understand the meaning.** Rewards then solve nothing and can be rather frustrating: "I want that reward, but I still don't know how to do something or why it makes sense."

- **Is a reward really the only meaningful thing for the child to get them motivated for an activity or task?** Then make sure the reward follows quickly. The more time between an activity or task and the reward, the harder it is to see the link between them.

- **Use rewards to celebrate successes and emphasize meaning rather than making them conditional.** ("If you do this, you'll get that.")

  HOME: *Give your child a reward after they do their homework without (too much) resistance. Rather than saying, "If you do your homework now, you will get an ice cream later," say,*

"You have done your homework well. Now not only can the teacher see how well you can do this, but also you know yourself whether you need to practice this more or have already mastered it. You even did that without much grumbling, so Mommy could already start dinner. That deserves an ice cream in a moment."

SCHOOL: *Rather than saying, "If you do your exercise now in silence, you can play a game on the computer later," we prefer, "You did the exercise all by yourself. Everyone worked in silence and you didn't disturb each other. As a result, we finished a little earlier now and have time to play a game on the computer."*

- **Think carefully ahead of time about what you can give as a reward and for what.** You'll read more about that in the last chapter of this book, on the need "encouragement."

STRATEGY 3: Do something for someone else

Autistic children also enjoy doing something for someone else, especially if it produces quick results and is a meaningful fulfilment of their free time. It is a way to highlight their connection and their competencies for a change.

- **A buddy system can often be reciprocal.** It is not just about another child or confidant doing something for the autistic child; it can also be the other way around. Perhaps an autistic child who does need some help on the playground can help another child in the classroom with something they are just strong at, such as math exercises or sorting books in an orderly fashion. Even when the (social) rush seems to get in the way of working on connection, doing something meaningful for another person can still generate a positive feeling.

  HOME: *Is playing during a party too difficult for your child? Maybe it's easier to bring snacks around or help prepare them in the kitchen.*

  SCHOOL: *Is the busyness of the classroom during craft time too difficult for the child? Then let the child do something else that works in the crowd and is part of the assignment, such as collecting paper scraps from other children or handing out pencils.*

- **Teach the child a game or activity that other children do not know.** This way, they can teach something new to others.

HOME: *Teach your child a household task that they can then teach to another family member.*

SCHOOL: *Have the child look up something about a class topic that they may then tell other children.*

- **Express gratitude when the child does something for you, and encourage them to do the same.** That is clear feedback on the positive feeling you give when you do something for another or that you get when another does something for you.

10

ENCOURAGEMENT

‘For autistic children, growing up is an elite sport. To keep that up, they need supporters.’

ENCOURAGEMENT
WHAT IS IT?

Growing up does not happen by itself. And certainly not if development is impaired by some kind of disability. Years ago, autism was sometimes called "a pervasive developmental disorder." Pervasive means "profound." Thus, autism would intrusively interfere with normal development. This does not at all mean that autistic children cannot develop, grow, and blossom. However, it does cost them much more effort than children without autism. For children without autism, growing up can be compared to playing recreational sports. It requires some effort, but not too much. It also comes almost naturally, and it is often fun. For autistic children, growing up is like playing an elite sport. It requires daily training, and they have to work hard. To keep it up, they need supporters. No top sports club can do without a fan club or supporters. In soccer, supporters are even called "the twelfth player," the extra player who stands off the field but is just as much needed to win as the team on the field. Without supporters, autistic children won't make it either.

Encouraging an autistic child meets that child's very first and most important need: to be understood. With compliments, you make it clear that you have an eye for the effort it requires to make progress, even though that progress is not always obvious. And the child is grateful for that.

You read earlier about the need for a positive self-esteem. Getting compliments and being surrounded by people who express their appreciation for what the child does is the breeding ground for a positive self-esteem. That positive self-esteem is the best

A supporter also provides connection. Facing challenges is easier when the child knows they are not alone.

weapon to deal with the difficulties and stresses of life. When supporters show their confidence in the child, the child is confident, which increases their resilience.

A supporter also provides connection, the other basic need of children with autism. Facing challenges succeeds a lot easier when the child knows they are not alone.

Jack's parents want him to learn to get around in traffic and go to school by bike. As a school, we think this is a meaningful learning goal, but Jack himself prefers to be brought by car. Then not only does he not have to make any physical effort—Jack hates moving—but in the safe cocoon of a car he is not bothered by the traffic. We found something that is more concrete and visual than verbal encouragement: We made a diary for Jack with a bicycle on the cover and below it the text "Tour de France." Every time Jack comes to school by bike, he gets a red sticker for that day. We explained what the sticker means: in the Tour de France, after each stage, a prize for combativeness is awarded to the cyclist who made an extra effort that day. That rider gets to ride the next day with a red jersey number instead of a white one. The red stickers are Jack's combativeness prize because he doesn't give up cycling to school.

PETER, SIXTH GRADE TEACHER

William plays a lot of computer games. This used to arouse our frustrations: he was sometimes puffed up when he survived some trek through the jungle with all his health points, and then he talked about it all the time while we didn't really know what he was talking about. Then we learned that such a trip takes quite a bit of time, perseverance, attention, and inventiveness. To be complimented on this success is therefore very important to William. "Wow, clever of you, William. That must not have been easy." Now, if we are interested in asking how he survives such a trip, his story is given a sincere place, and we find that he feels good.

KATIA, MOM OF WILLIAM, TWELVE YEARS OLD

WIN
YOU WIN!

HOW CAN YOU SUPPORT THIS NEED?

STRATEGY 1: Compliment concretely

Because the brain of an autistic child has no real talent for inferring things from context, it only becomes clear what a compliment is and for whom exactly it is intended when you state it very explicitly and concretely.

- **Make it clear that you are complimenting.** With younger children, a little theater can sometimes help to highlight the value ("Great! Fantastic! Super well done!"), but be careful about exaggerating with somewhat older children. It can make your compliment just barely believable.

- **Don't overdo it when you give a compliment:** that can lead to unrealistic, overly positive self-esteem. Autistic children sometimes understand things rather absolutely or literally. Make sure your compliment is consistent with what the child did.

- **Contrary to what you sometimes hear, many autistic children can cope with figurative language,** provided they know it is not meant literally and they—like all other children—have learned the figurative meaning. Expressions such as, "You light up the room," or, "I take my hat off to that," can help clarify your encouragement because they are visual.

- **Also clarify why or what you are complimenting about.** As specifically as possible, name what you are complimenting or encouraging.

HOME: *"You cleaned up your room. That makes me happy," "You're ready to go to school on time. That deserves a thumbs-up!"*

SCHOOL: *"Very clever of you to let another student choose which game to play," "Wow, were you able to complete all the exercises by yourself? Kudos!"*

STRATEGY 2: Think about what you encourage

You can compliment autistic children for very different things:

- Their personality or character traits, e.g., "Your honesty adorns you."
- Their appearance, for example, "How pretty you look with your short-cut hair."
- A result or goal they achieved, e.g., "I'm proud of you for getting your swimming badge."
- The efforts they made, e.g., "Kudos to you for the many hours you studied for this test."
- The way they handled something, e.g., "I think it's great that you remembered to ask for an explanation when you didn't quite understand the assignment."
- What they mean to someone, e.g., "Your humor creates fun moments in class. You make the other students happy." (This kind of compliment, by the way, is very important in light of the need for meaning.)

Here are a few tips for making your encouragement meaningful to a child with autism:

- **Don't go encouraging several things at once:** AND the effort AND the result AND the strategy. Then an autistic child with autism cannot see the woods for the trees. If you encourage for one thing, it makes the compliment more precise and therefore stronger.

- **Vary what you encourage for.** If you only give compliments for achieving a goal or result, it might take a long time for the child to get a compliment. The child then gets no understanding or encouragement for all the efforts they are making in the meantime.

- **You often hear that it is best to avoid compliments for the end result because they promote achievement or can put pressure on children**, but also because they can provoke insecurity and fear of failure because goals cannot always be achieved (instantly). On the other hand, you should always encourage children for the efforts they make. Such compliments certainly belong in the arsenal of compliments you give, but for an autistic child, it is not nice to always hear "You tried hard" without also once succeeding in that for which they put so much effort. Therefore, in your compliments, it is best to link effort with progress: "Well done: you have practiced a lot, and now you can already write your name."

- **Don't just compliment what you as a parent or teacher think is important.** Each child has his or her own goals too.

- **In your compliment, emphasize the child's own part in their success.** Sometimes children do minimize this: "It only worked because the teacher gave more time," or, "It would never have worked without the step-by-step plan." In such cases, make the child's part in the success explicit by saying, "You used that extra time very well!" or, "You followed that step-by-step plan meticulously."

STRATEGY 3: Collect compliments

Just as previous successes do not always stick in the memory of autistic children, they also seem to be quick to forget compliments. Make sure the compliments last by literally shaping and collecting them.

- **Images help to make your appreciation visual.** This keeps the compliments clear, and the child literally sees what they can be proud of. Others can also see those compliments, and that creates connection.

  HOME: *Create a "compliment tree." Leaves can be notes with compliments.*

  SCHOOL: *Make Facebook-sized thumbs-up visible in the classroom (but with the clear message that it is not a competition).*

- **You can also create a compliment journal with the child.** In it, you record one (or two or three) compliment each day. To teach the child to look at themself positively, you can ask them to also give themself one compliment a day. Then, if they ever doubt themself, the compliment diary can be the necessary boost. You can get inspiration from the glass jar of successes from the chapter on the need for "positive self-esteem."

being seen
affection
support
concern
safety

"STRONG MAKERS *IN* AUTISM"

Peter Vermeulen and **Kobe Vanroy** are educational staff at "sterkmakers *in* autisme" (literal translation: "strong makers *in* autism"). This Belgian organization sensitizes and informs through activities that teach about autism and all it entails. With their work, they want to empower anyone with a heart for autism and an eye for inclusion.

Because not everyone processes information in the same way, the "strong makers in autism" are building a diverse range of activities to suit many ways of learning. We value reliable and accessible information about autism, as we strive to be always clear and predictable, sometimes with a wink, but each time in cooperation with those most concerned: people with autism.

Under the name "Autism in Context", Peter also presents internationally, mostly on wellbeing in autism. Kobe is specialized in teaching about autism friendly education.